SKILLS & VALUES:
PROPERTY LAW

SKILLS & VALUES: PROPERTY LAW

Brian D. Shannon
Charles B. "Tex" Thornton Professor of Law
Texas Tech University School of Law

Gerry W. Beyer
Governor Preston E. Smith Regents Professor of Law
Texas Tech University School of Law

ISBN: 978–1–4224–8047–2

Library of Congress Cataloging-in-Publication Data

Shannon, Brian D., 1958-
Skills & values : property law / Brian Shannon, Gerry W. Beyer.
p. cm.
ISBN 978-1-4224-8047-2
1. Real property--United States--Problems, exercises, etc. 2. Personal property--United States--Problems, exercises, etc. I. Beyer, Gerry W. II. Title.
KF570.Z9S53 2012
346.7304--dc23

2012035493

This publication is designed to provide authoritative information in regard to the subject matter covered. It is sold with the understanding that the publisher is not engaged in rendering legal, accounting, or other professional services. If legal advice or other expert assistance is required, the services of a competent professional should be sought.

NOTE TO USERS
To ensure that you are using the latest materials available in this area, please be sure to periodically check the LexisNexis Law School web site for downloadable updates and supplements at www.lexisnexis.com/lawschool.

Editorial Offices
121 Chanlon Rd., New Providence, NJ 07974 (908) 464-6800
201 Mission St., San Francisco, CA 94105-1831 (415) 908-3200
www.lexisnexis.com

MATTHEW◆BENDER

(2012–Pub.3311)

Introduction

These materials were created as a means to assist you in incorporating practical lawyering skills into your substantive Property class. From our many years of teaching Property and other law school courses, we have found that students yearn for practical examples of the often abstract principles that are being studied. The exercises in this book are intended to give you real world contexts for the underlying doctrine that you are studying. Moreover, we have found that our students often have a much better grasp of the cases and subject matter when they can see it in the context of "real" practice. The exercises are also intended to get you thinking about good lawyering.

Each chapter in this book includes one or more stand-alone exercises that include fact patterns based on topics generally covered in a first-year Property course. In total, this book includes fourteen chapters. For those of you who are taking a one-semester Property course, this structure allows your professor to select one or more exercises from each chapter during each week of a typical, fourteen-week semester. For those of you in a year-long Property class, your professor might assign the problems in each chapter over every two-week period. The subject matter of each chapter is intended to cover most of the major topics encountered in a traditional first-year Property class. The various exercises require you to engage in many of the practice skills necessary to handle Property issues in the "real world," such as document drafting, analyzing client problems (both factual and legal analysis), client letters, statutory interpretation, litigation strategy, negotiation, ethics, and general problem-solving.

Each chapter also includes a "self-study" component. Here, we provide our approach to the various exercises, or an identification of key topics/issues that we believe should be considered for each problem. These are not intended to be *the answers*, because good lawyering is contextual and requires creativity, individuality, and effort. Different lawyers will often approach the same problems in different manners. That does not mean one approach is right and the other is wrong. We urge you to consider and craft your own solutions. To that end, we discourage you from peeking ahead at the self-study sections until after you have endeavored to complete the various exercises. We do not want to unduly narrow your thinking and creativity. In fact, you might come up with a more appropriate or clever solution than ours!

E-Materials

This *Skills & Values* book is enhanced by a **LexisNexis Webcourse** which will give you access to online content tailored to the use of this book. Your professor will provide you with instructions on how to enroll in this Webcourse. The online content includes an array of resources to help you consider and address the various exercises. These include, for example, videotapes of mock client interviews, online resources for researching deed records and tax appraisal information, and links to key cases, statutes, ordinances, law review articles, practitioner's papers, sample form documents, relevant websites, media stories, etc. These e-materials also include items to assist in self-assessment of the work completed on certain problem sets such as interactive forms. For some problems, we have suggested that you apply the statutes or law of one or more designated states. In other problems, we have identified some other source of local law or general law ranging from

Introduction

ordinances to sections of uniform laws or Restatement provisions. Your professor, however, might opt to have you consider one or more of the exercises under the law of your jurisdiction.

Organization of Each Chapter

Each chapter contains:

- An introduction that puts the chapter within the context of actual, day-to-day practice.
- A listing of skills involved in accomplishing each exercise.
- The estimated time for completing each task in the exercise(s), indicated by the icon below, each representing 15 minutes.

- The level of difficulty, represented by 1-5 "Black diamonds," as indicated by the icon set forth below.

- Your role in the exercise(s).
- "The exercise" section.
- A reminder about the online e-materials that accompany the exercise(s).

It is our hope that your work on these exercises will help illuminate the underlying principles of Property law through practical applications. More importantly, we want to assist you in making a challenging subject more understandable, more realistic, less dry, and more fun! Just remember, although most of you are now first-year law students, it will not be very long before you will be working with clients on an everyday basis, and we want you to be ready to be outstanding professionals who make it their business to be committed, ethical problem-solvers.

The authors would like to thank Mikela Bryant (J.D., Texas Tech University School of Law) and Bryan Jinks (J.D., The Ohio State University Moritz College of Law) for their stellar assistance in preparing these materials.

TABLE OF CONTENTS

Chapter 1

ACQUISITION: FOUND PROPERTY

INTRODUCTION

A person may acquire possession of personal property through a variety of mechanisms. The six most common are:

1. Find,

2. Borrow (e.g., holding as a consensual bailee, either as a favor from a relative or friend or by renting from a business),

3. Purchase,

4. Take in an unauthorized manner (civil conversion or criminal theft),

5. Benefit from another person's mistaken improvement to your property (accession), and

6. Receive gratuitously

    a. From a living donor (inter vivos gift or gift causa mortis), or

    b. From a dead donor (heir under intestate succession, beneficiary under a will, recipient under a non-probate transfer such as a life insurance policy or survivorship rights on a bank account).

This chapter focuses on finding, the first of these acquisition methods. Chapter 2 covers acquisition by way of gift. The purchase and rental of personal property is generally covered in a course on Contracts or Sales while the purchase of land is the subject of Chapters 9-11. Likewise, taking in an unauthorized manner is the subject of other courses; conversion is covered in Torts, and theft in Criminal Law.

A person is a *finder* if the person rightfully acquires possession of personal property that does not already belong to the person. Although the finder has rightful possession of the property, that is, the finder did not convert or steal the property, the finder does not have ownership of the property. Generally, a finder's rights are superior to everyone except the true owner, but there are some important exceptions. And, under some circumstances, it is possible that the finder's rightful possession will morph into true ownership.

The first step in analyzing a found property case is to classify the property. This is a highly significant step, because different rules may apply to the different classifications of property. Individuals attempting to have priority to the property may claim the property belongs in the category with the rules most favorable to them. The five traditional classifications of found property are as follows:

1. *First occupant property.* First occupant property is property over which no one has previously had ownership. A capture of a wild animal is a common example of first occupant property.

2. *Lost property.* Lost property is property over which the owner no longer has possession because of casual, involuntary, unconscious, or careless conduct. At the time of the loss, the owner is unaware that he or she no longer has possession.

3. *Misplaced or mislaid property.* Misplaced or mislaid property is property over which the owner no longer has possession because he or she intentionally placed it somewhere, but then unintentionally left the property behind.

4. *Abandoned property.* Abandoned property is property over which the owner has intentionally relinquished possession, but not in favor of any specific person, and has no intention of regaining possession in the future. In other words, the owner threw away the property.

5. *Treasure trove.* Treasure trove originally included gold, silver, and similar property which the Romans buried or otherwise secreted in England, erroneously believing that they would return for it and which was later found by English citizens. In modern times, the term refers to money and similar property which has no known owner and which is concealed in the ground or other hiding place.

The second step is to determine who should have continued possession of the found property. Several claimants might assert the right to possess, such as the finder, the owner of the land on which the property was found, the finder's employer if the finder found the property while on the job, the government, and, of course, the owner of the property. Generally, the finder can retain first occupant property and abandoned property. The finder can also retain lost property unless the claimant is the true owner or the finder gained possession of the property during the course of the finder's employment, in which case many courts give the finder's employer the superior right of possession. Because the owner might remember where the owner mislaid or misplaced property, the owner of the land on which this property was found normally has the superior right of possession. The finder traditionally could retain treasure trove unless the government had superior rights. Many modern decisions relegate the classification of treasure trove to history and treat this type of property either as lost or mislaid, whichever is more strongly supported by the facts.

The third step is to determine whether the finder's possessory rights will transform into ownership if the true owner cannot be found or the law eliminates the true owner's rights. Typically, if the true owner claims the property, the true owner may regain possession from the finder, property owner, or government. The true owner's rights may, however, be lost if the property cannot be recovered because the statute of limitations for conversion has run or the possessor has obtained ownership via adverse possession. About one-half of the states have legislation which provides procedures that finders must follow and contains rules for determining when and if the finder becomes the owner.

EXERCISE 1-1

GENERAL DESCRIPTION OF EXERCISE: Examine a variety of found property situations and determine who has superior rights.

SKILLS INVOLVED: Fact analysis and development, communication skills with clients, negotiation with counsel for opposing party.

PARTICIPANTS NEEDED: Tasks 1 and 2 are group exercises with teams of equal numbers of students on each team. Tasks 3 and 4 are independent exercises.

ESTIMATED TIME REQUIRED:

Task 1: Two hours to watch video and prepare client letter.

Task 2: One hour to meet with opposing counsel and attempt to resolve the issue.

Task 3: Two hours to study provided statute and prepare client letter.

Task 4: Two hours to research applicable law and prepare client letter.

LEVEL OF DIFFICULTY (1-5):

ROLE IN EXERCISE: You are the attorney for the finders of property. You have established a reputation in the community as the "go to" person to resolve issues dealing with found property. Each of your clients would like to retain the property they have found if the true owner does not make a timely claim to the property.

THE EXERCISE

TASK 1: You and your teammates represent either Alex Popov or Patrick Hayashi. Each one claims ownership of the baseball Barry Bonds hit for home run number seventy-three on October 7, 2001. Alex claims the ball belongs to him because he had it in his glove and lost it only because it was dislodged when a mob of spectators tackled him. On the other hand, Patrick claims the ball is his because Alex never had actual possession of the ball and at the end of the mêlée, he walked away with the ball. To obtain the facts you need to make your arguments, watch the trailer for the movie *Up for Grabs* to view the actual events as they unfolded. The link can be found on the **LexisNexis Webcourse** for this chapter. Prepare a letter to your client which explains his situation.

APPLICABLE LAW:

Use general principles of common law.

TASK 2: Meet with counsel for the other side and attempt to resolve the situation described in Task 1 without resorting to time-consuming and costly litigation.

TASK 3: Julie James, a freshman at Big State University, has come to you a few months before the end of her first year in college. Julie is distraught; six months ago, she lost her most precious possession — an antique diamond bracelet — at a hair salon near campus. Julie believes the bracelet fell off while she enjoyed a day of pampering during Homecoming Week in November. She was so caught up in the excitement of the day that she did not notice the bracelet was missing until she got home from the salon. By that time, the salon had already closed and would not be open until Monday morning. When Julie returned on Monday, none of the employees admitted to having seen the bracelet. The owner of the salon told Julie she would keep an eye out for it. It is now early April, and Julie recently returned to the same salon for a routine cut and color. While being shampooed, Julie noticed that the stylist at the next wash bin was wearing an antique diamond bracelet on her right wrist which was identical to the bracelet she lost. The stylist, who had only been working at the salon since January, told Julie she found the bracelet underneath the cabinet at her assigned space. She had cleaned her work station out a few weeks ago and found the bracelet amidst hair clippings in a hard-to-reach nook under the counter. She assumed the bracelet was just a piece a pretty costume jewelry that the previous stylist or one of that stylist's clients had lost. She saw no reason to look for the owner at the time. Although Julie has now told the stylist that the bracelet was hers, the new stylist refuses to return it to her.

Julie has come to you for advice. She has not told her mother she lost the bracelet in November and does not want to move home in May without it. Not only does it have enormous sentimental value, it is also worth $2,500.00. Write a letter to Julie discussing your understanding of the law and what you believe her options are in regards to retrieving the bracelet. Make sure to include all potential outcomes.

APPLICABLE LAW:

Found personal property[1]

(1) Notwithstanding any other provision of law, any person who finds money or goods valued at one hundred dollars ($100) or more, excepting firearms, explosives or other deadly weapons shall, if the owner of the money or goods is unknown, give written notice of the finding within ten (10) days to the county clerk of the county in which the money or goods were found. Within twenty (20) days after the date of the finding, the person who finds such money or goods shall cause to be published in a newspaper of general circulation in the county a notice of the finding once each week for two (2) consecutive weeks. Each such notice shall state:

(a) A general description of the money or goods found;

(b) The address and telephone number of the county clerk's office; and

(c) The final date by which such money or goods must be claimed.

(2) If no person establishes ownership of the money or goods prior to the expiration of three (3) months from the date of the notice to the county clerk, as provided in subsection (1) of this section, the person who found such money or goods shall be the rightful owner thereof.

(3) (a) If any person who finds money or goods valued at one hundred dollars ($100) or more, excepting firearms, explosives or other deadly weapons fails to comply with the provisions of subsection (1) of this section, such person shall be liable to the county for the money or goods or for the value of such money or goods.

(b) Upon forfeiture of the money or goods, or the value of such money or goods, as provided in this subsection, the county treasurer shall hold the money or goods or their value for the owner and shall publish in a newspaper of general circulation in the county a notice of the finding once each week for two (2) consecutive weeks. Each such notice shall state:

(i) A general description of the money or goods found;

(ii) The address and telephone number of the county treasurer's office; and

(iii) The final date by which such money or goods must be claimed.

(c) If the owner does not reclaim the money or goods within three (3) months after the date of first publication of the notice by the county treasurer, the owner forfeits any rights to the money or goods or the value thereof and:

(i) If money, such money shall be placed in the general fund of the county for payment of the general operating expenses of the county; or

(ii) If goods, such goods shall be delivered to the sheriff of the county and sold at public auction. The proceeds of the sale of such goods shall be applied first to the costs of the sale and the remainder shall be placed in the general fund of the county for the payment of the general operating expenses of the county.

---

[1] Adapted from Idaho Code § 55-405.

(4) An owner of money or goods found by another person who establishes a claim to such money or goods within the time period specified in this section shall have restitution of such money or goods, or their value, upon payment to the finder or the county treasurer, as applicable, of all costs and charges incurred in the finding, giving of notice, and care and custody of such money or goods.

TASK 4: During renovation operations that were being done on Juan's house and surrounding property, construction crews unearthed two large duffle bags, both filled with burlap bags of cash. Juan is not sure what he should do with the money. The large tattooed workers are pestering him for the money. The suits from the construction company are also showing up demanding that Juan turn over the money. There are also rumors that in the 1930s, bank robbers hid a large stash of money similar to this one in the area and that this might be it. The bank is still in operation having survived the robbery and the Depression due to skillful management. Prepare a letter to Juan outlining his rights and obligations.

APPLICABLE LAW:

Use the law of the state in which you intend to practice.

Chapter 2

ACQUISITION: GIFTS

INTRODUCTION

This chapter will focus on problems relating to gifts of either personal or real property. In your Contracts course you learned (or will learn) that a promise to make a gift is generally unenforceable. For enforcement of a promise there must be either bargained-for consideration or substantial detrimental reliance on an otherwise unenforceable promise. Thus, a person who has made a promise to make a gift typically has the ability to change his or her mind prior to any promised transfer of property (and can thereby revoke). Under concepts of Property law, however, a completed gift — as opposed to the mere promise to make a gift — is recognized as a binding transfer of property (and generally cannot be revoked).

The most common type of gift is a lifetime transfer of property from a person making the gift (the donor) to a person receiving the gift (the donee). This *inter vivos* gift (*i.e.*, a gift "between the living") encompasses the typical holiday, birthday, wedding, and anniversary present. The three key elements for the validity of an *inter vivos* gift are (1) donative intent, (2) delivery, and (3) acceptance. More specifically: (1) did the donor *intend* an immediate transfer of property by gift? (2) Did the donor actually *deliver* the object of the gift to the donee (and thereby relinquish dominion and control)? And (3) did the donee *accept* the object of the gift? Moreover, the acceptance of something of value is generally presumed; so, issues regarding acceptance of a gift do not often arise. In addition, most gifts occur between family members or friends, and typically transpire without any dispute. When disputes arise, however, they most often involve issues regarding the elements of donative intent or delivery.

The element of *delivery* can be satisfied by any of three different means: (1) *actual* or *manual* delivery (in effect, handing over the property); (2) *symbolic* delivery; or (3) *constructive* delivery. An *actual* or *manual* delivery of property is typically required when it is practicable; for example, Diane Donor hands Darleen Donee a birthday present of a ruby ring. In contrast, had Diane simply stated orally or put in writing, "I am giving you a ruby ring for your birthday," delivery would be lacking at that point.

More explanation is warranted regarding the latter two types of delivery. With regard to *symbolic* delivery, some items might be too large or cumbersome for actual delivery. Other types of property might not be readily accessible (for example, stock certificates that are in the donor's safe deposit box). In those cases, courts have recognized as valid the handing over of a writing that declares a gift of the subject property; for example a letter handed from the donor to the donee stating, "I give you my king-size, canopy brass bed. s/Dave Donor"; or "I hereby give you my 100 shares of Acme stock; the stock certificates are in my lock box at the First State Bank. s/Darla Donor." These writings could be viewed as symbolic delivery of the actual property, and many courts will recognize this type of symbolic delivery when actual delivery is impracticable (or even impossible). Symbolic delivery is not limited to this type of writing. Something like a photograph of a large item may be recognized as symbolic delivery, as well. Additionally, symbolic delivery is the accepted approach for gifts of real property. It would obviously be impossible to hand-deliver 100 acres of land. Accordingly, the handing over of a duly executed deed serves as symbolic delivery.

In contrast, for a valid *constructive* delivery, the donor transfers something to the donee that gives the donee access to or control over the property that is being donated. For example, for a large locked desk or large safe, the donor might hand the keys to the donee. The donor would not be able to physically hand the desk over to the donee, so the keys serve as a form of constructive delivery. The delivery of keys to a small item (such as a small lockbox) might not be recognized as a valid constructive delivery, however, if it is readily practicable to hand over the box itself.

A gift of a check raises interesting questions about delivery. Suppose that Diane wants to make a gift to Dan and hands him a check for $100. Diane no doubt intended to make a gift, and Dan probably believes that he has received a gift. But, what if Diane dies prior to Dan's having the check cashed? The traditional and likely still majority rule is that the gift funds have not been delivered. In theory, Diane still has dominion and control over the funds until the check is cashed. There is some contrasting authority, however, by courts that have upheld valid gifts of checks on facts similar to these given the donor's clear intent and delivery of the check.

Certain types of gifts can be subject to a condition. A good example is the gift of an engagement ring. In most jurisdictions, this gift is viewed as being coupled with an implied condition that the marriage takes place. The gift then becomes absolute (and no longer subject to the implied condition) upon the conclusion of the wedding.

In addition to *inter vivos* gifts, people also make gifts in contemplation of death. Traditionally, these have been *testamentary* gifts governed by the law of wills. Gifts set forth in a will involve transfers of property not at present, but after the death of the donor — identified typically as the testator. You will have an opportunity to study the law of wills in an upper level course, but wills statutes in most states require formalities such as a writing signed by the testator, whose signature is witnessed by at least two disinterested other people. Moreover, in contrast with a completed *inter vivos* gift, while a person is still alive, she may revoke an existing will, amend an existing will with properly executed codicils, or entirely replace a will with a newly executed will.

An intermediate type of gift is known as the gift *causa mortis*. Like a will, this type of gift is also made in contemplation of death. In contrast to a will, however, the gift is made immediately while the donor is still alive, as opposed to a transfer after death. Like an *inter vivos* gift, the gift *causa mortis* requires the elements of intent, delivery, and acceptance. But, in addition, there is a fourth element requiring the donor's contemplation or anticipation of imminent death (or expectation of immediately approaching death). Just as with an *inter vivos* gift, the gift *causa mortis* is effective immediately upon transfer of the property. In contrast, however, to the *inter vivos* gift, if the donor of a gift *causa mortis* survives and does not die as had been anticipated, in most states the gift is automatically revoked. (Some states alternatively require the donor to revoke the gift, but even in those states the gift *causa mortis* is revocable.) Of course, disputes can arise as to whether the surviving donor intended the gift to be an *inter vivos* gift, which is irrevocable, or a gift *causa mortis*, which is revocable — either automatically in most states or at the election of the donor in other states.

EXERCISE 2-1

GENERAL DESCRIPTION OF EXERCISE: Addressing legal questions that arise involving gifts.

SKILLS INVOLVED: Fact analysis and development, case research and analysis, creative problem solving, preparation for and participation in negotiations and mediation, drafting of agreements.

PARTICIPANTS NEEDED: Task 1 is an individual project, and Tasks 2 and 3 are collaborative and require four and five students, respectively.

ESTIMATED TIME REQUIRED:

Task 1: 45 minutes

Task 2: 30 minutes to prepare and 45-60 minutes to mediate

Task 3: 30 minutes to analyze and 45-60 minutes to negotiate

LEVEL OF DIFFICULTY (1-5):

ROLES IN EXERCISE: You are acting as a lawyer for a party as identified in the various tasks. Some of you will serve as a mediator in Task 2.

THE EXERCISE: 2-1

Your firm's client is Ann Akers. Ann is a 27-year-old software design engineer with both a bachelor's and master's degree from the Minnetoba Institute of Technology. Ann has been employed by Minntech, a high-tech corporation located in Minnetoba City, Minnetoba, for the last three years, and she earns just over $100,000 per year. For the last three years, Ann has been in a serious dating relationship with Bob Bass, who is a 28-year-old Ph.D. student in English Literature at the University of Minnetoba in Minnetoba City. Bob is set to complete his studies and dissertation by the end of May. Three months ago, the couple became engaged, and they have set a wedding date of June 26.

TASK 1: Assume that your law practice is in Minnetoba City, which is located in the state of Minnetoba. You are a first-year associate at the firm. Ann happens to be an old friend of yours from high school. Ann has just met with you, and she was very upset. About two weeks ago, Bob announced to her that he had been hired for a job as an Assistant Professor in the English Department at the University of Calitoba, in College City, Calitoba. The job is set to begin next September. College City is located around 700 miles from Minnetoba City, and it is a small college town. There is essentially no high tech industry in the town, and it is highly unlikely that Ann could find work comparable to her current job or suitable to her skills and ability. Ann is quite broken-hearted. Bob had not told her anything about his job application process, but explained that he had wanted to surprise Ann only once he obtained a teaching position. Last week, Ann decided to break off the engagement and told Bob that even though she loved him with her whole heart, she just could not give up her job and move to College City. Bob told her that he thought she would be happy about his new teaching job and that she would want to go with him to College City. Bob was both angry and hurt. He immediately asked Ann to return the diamond and sapphire engagement ring that he gave her three months ago, as well as a pair of diamond earrings that he gave her for her last birthday just over six months ago. Ann has not yet returned the engagement ring or the diamond earrings. During your meeting with her, Ann asked you whether she had to return them. Because she is feeling so hurt and upset, she is thinking about keeping them. She has told you that the engagement ring has a value of $8,000, and the diamond earrings are worth $2,000. Your task is to review the cases and materials on the **LexisNexis Webcourse** for this task and prepare for a follow-up meeting with Ann to discuss her options.

TASK 2: Assume that several weeks have passed since your prior meetings with Ann (as described in Task 1 above). Bob has decided not to press his claim for the return of the diamond earrings, but he has insisted on a return of the engagement ring. Ann has refused to do so. Bob has now retained counsel of his own. Rather than filing a lawsuit, however, Bob's attorney has requested that the matter be set for a mediation session at the local Minnetoba County Dispute Resolution Center. Ann has reluctantly agreed to participate in the mediation. Located on the **LexisNexis Webcourse** for this part of the exercise are short videos of client interviews between Ann, Bob, and their respective counsel. Working in pairs, some of you will serve as counsel for Ann and some of you will represent Bob. There is also a link to information for those of you who are designated by your professor to serve as the mediator. After reviewing and considering the linked material for your role, you are to (1) develop your plan and strategy for the mediation session; (2) participate in a mediation — your professor will identify the match-ups for these sessions; and (3) draft a memorandum of agreement if you are able to reach a settlement during the mediation.

TASK 3: For purposes of this task, assume that unlike the facts set forth in Tasks 1 and 2, shortly after their break-up, Ann and Bob reconciled. Ann's employer, Minntech, agreed to let Ann keep her job at her current salary level, but to allow her to telecommute from College City. The company will require her to return to headquarters in Minnetoba City once every two weeks, but Minntech committed to pay the travel expenses. Both Ann and Bob were ecstatic, and they moved to College City in the latter part of May, shortly after Bob's graduation. Given that they had to move 700 miles from two different households to a newly purchased home, they opted to postpone their wedding date to August 10, just two weeks prior to the start of Bob's academic year. Over the July 4 holiday weekend, they hosted a combined housewarming and engagement party for family and friends. Among their many guests was Bob's Uncle Ned. Ned, a very successful periodontist, drove up to the house in his two-year old, red BMW convertible coupe. Both Ann and Bob stared admiringly at the car when Ned arrived, and Ned happened to notice. Ned quickly exclaimed, "I hadn't picked out either a housewarming or a wedding present for you two, yet. In fact, it's high time for me to buy a new one of these cars. Let me give you this one to celebrate your engagement!" Much to Ann's and Bob's astonishment, Ned then held his car keys aloft, jingled them loudly, and tossed them to the couple from across the driveway. Ann and Bob were obviously thrilled. After the party, they gave Ned a ride to his home (approximately 15 miles away on the outskirts of College City), and they drove the BMW home. The next week, Bob sold his fifteen-year old Honda sedan.

All was well until the last week of July. Ann and Bob, feeling overwhelmed about trying to get the wedding pulled together so shortly after their move, mutually decided to cancel their wedding plans. Still very much in love, however, they decided that they would simply live together. They let their friends and family know, and returned many of the wedding gifts that they had already received. They did not, however, want to part with the red BMW. They sent Uncle Ned an e-mail to let him know that the wedding had been cancelled, but they did not mention the red BMW at all. Uncle Ned wrote back and demanded that they return the BMW. He said, "Now that you're not getting married, I need you to return the BMW to me at your earliest convenience. In fact, it's not really yours anyway because I have never signed over the certificate of title. I also kept another set of keys." Ann and Bob have thus far refused. Ned hired an attorney, and now Ann and Bob have also retained counsel. The car has an estimated value of $40,000.

Located on the **LexisNexis Webcourse** for this part of the exercise are (1) some relevant legal materials, (2) instructions for counsel for Ned, and (3) instructions for counsel for Ann and Bob. Your professor will assign you to work in pairs and for each pair to represent either Ned or Ann and Bob. After reviewing and considering the legal issues and the guidance from your client(s), you are to (1) develop your plan and strategy for a negotiation session with counsel for the opposing side; (2) engage in a negotiation with the pair of students who are representing the opposing side — your professor will identify the match-ups for the negotiation sessions; and (3) draft a memorandum of agreement if you are able to reach a settlement during the negotiation session.

EXERCISE 2-2

GENERAL DESCRIPTION OF EXERCISE: Addressing legal questions that arise with respect to gifts of real property.

SKILLS INVOLVED: Fact, case, and statutory analysis, creative problem solving, use of forms and resource materials to prepare deeds.

PARTICIPANTS NEEDED: These tasks are collaborative and require two students for each.

ESTIMATED TIME REQUIRED:

Task 1: 30 minutes

Task 2: One hour — 30 minutes to prepare and 30 minutes to draft

Task 3: One hour — 30 minutes to analyze and 30 minutes to prepare a letter

LEVEL OF DIFFICULTY (1-5):

ROLES IN EXERCISE: You are acting as a lawyer for the parties as identified in the various tasks.

THE EXERCISE: 2-2

Mabel is a 70-year old widow who has survived her late husband Elmer for six years. Mabel is the owner of a nice home in the Green Pastures subdivision of Minnetoba City, Minnetoba. She also owns a 640-acre farm in rural, southeastern Minnetoba that has been in her family for over 100 years. The farm includes a large turkey production operation, and is known as Gobbler-acre. Mabel only visits the farm a few times per year, and she has hired a tenant/supervisor to handle day-to-day operations and upkeep. Mabel has two grown children, Angie and Burl. Angie is a veterinarian and lives in southeast Minnetoba not very far from the farm. Burl is a lawyer who works as the deputy general counsel for a federal agency in Washington. Because Angie has long loved the farm, and Burl has indicated that he has no interest in ever returning to Minnetoba on a permanent basis, Mabel recently decided to give the farm to Angie. Mabel hired an attorney to prepare a deed of gift for the farm, and Mabel gave the deed to Angie a few months ago. (A link to this deed is located on the **LexisNexis Webcourse** for this chapter.)

TASK 1:   Mabel and Angie recently learned that the owners of a neighboring farm had successfully drilled a producing natural gas well on their land. The exploration company has indicated that it is likely that successful gas wells can be drilled on Gobbler-acre, as well. Mabel is concerned. She was happy to provide the farm to Angie given Burl's lack of interest, but she would have preferred to retain any rights to royalties on gas production as a source of income. Plus, Mabel believes that both Angie and Burl should ultimately inherit that type of income stream equally after she dies. Accordingly, Mabel asked Angie to give her back the deed to Gobbler-acre, and Angie did so. Mabel has now come to see you and asked you to draw up a new deed by which Mabel retains all of the mineral rights and only transfers to Angie the surface estate. First, is this the appropriate approach to carrying out Mabel's wishes? If not, describe an approach that will accomplish Mabel's goals. After reviewing the e-materials located on the **LexisNexis Webcourse** for this task, work with a classmate to discuss and analyze the issues. Draft the appropriate deed(s) to address these new facts. You may assume that Angie is entirely agreeable with Mabel's stated desires, and she has waived any potential conflict of interest in your preparation of the necessary instrument(s).

TASK 2:   Assume that several years have passed. Mabel is now 73 years old, and she has recently had some significant health problems. Assume also that Mabel and Angie ultimately decided not to go through with any type of re-conveyance of the mineral interests in Gobbler-acre. Accordingly, Angie owns a fee simple interest in all of Gobbler-acre (both the surface and mineral estates). Recently, Mabel has consulted with a lawyer regarding a new will. Other than her home in Green Pastures and some personal and household items, Mabel has a very small estate. She is primarily living on social security and annuity payments from her late husband's retirement plan. After meeting with her lawyer and learning about the surprising costs and complexities of the probate process in Minnetoba, Mabel has decided to deed the property to her two adult children, Angie and Burl, now but to remain in the home as long as she is able. Her lawyer told her that she could deed remainder interests in the home to Angie and Burl, but retain the house for the rest of her life. Although she was not quite certain what that means, it sounded like a good plan to her if it would help her children avoid the cumbersome aspects of probate. Your task is to review the information set forth in the e-materials on the **LexisNexis Webcourse** for this chapter, and draft a deed to carry out Mabel's stated wishes. If you were Mabel's counsel, are there any concerns about such a transfer that you would want to advise her? You may work with another classmate to undertake this task.

TASK 3: Suppose that shortly after meeting with Mabel regarding the underlying facts in Task 2, you discovered that the Minnetoba legislature had only recently enacted the Uniform Real Property Transfer on Death Act. (A link to this Uniform Act is included on the **LexisNexis Webcourse** for this task.) After reviewing the statute, you have decided that a revocable deed with a transfer on death provision as authorized by the new statute would better serve your client's stated wishes. After discussing this option with Mabel, she has authorized you to prepare such a deed. Your task is to review the legislation and prepare a revocable deed of Mabel's home to Angie and Burl that will be effective only upon Mabel's death.

Chapter 3

CO-OWNERSHIP OF PROPERTY: REAL PROPERTY

INTRODUCTION

It is quite common for two or more individuals to own concurrent interests in the same parcel of real property. For example, spouses will typically purchase a home together. Also, individual property owners will often transfer or devise real property to a class of children or siblings. (For example, O leaves Blackacre in her will "to my children A and B.") There were three types of common law co-ownership of property that remain important today. These are (1) the tenancy in common, (2) the joint tenancy with right of survivorship, and (3) the tenancy by the entirety.[1] Additionally, more than one individual can have ownership interests in a parcel of real property, but then have consecutive rights of possession. For example, if O transfers property "to A for life, then to B," A would have a life estate interest and B would own the remainder interest (more precisely, a vested remainder in fee simple). Issues pertaining to consecutive possessory rights and future interests will be addressed in Chapter 7. This chapter, however, addresses concurrent ownership.

Today, if a party transfers property to two or more persons via a conveyance or devise such as "to A and B" or "to A, B, and C," the form of ownership is likely a *tenancy in common*. Each tenant in common has an undivided interest in the entire parcel, but a fractional ownership interest. In the first example, A has a 50% undivided interest in the property, and A has a 33.33% undivided interest in the second example. Each of the co-owners has the right to transfer or devise that person's share to another person. There are no rights of survivorship held by any owner. Moreover, each of the co-owners has the right to use or possess the entire parcel notwithstanding that the person owns only a fractional share or even just a minority ownership interest. Not surprisingly, issues and disputes can arise among the co-owners.

By way of contrast, the *joint tenancy with right of survivorship*, is a form of co-ownership of property in which each of the co-owners — like the name implies — has a right of survivorship. Thus, like the tenancy in common, each of the co-owners has an undivided ownership and possessory interest in the whole of the property; but,

---

[1] There were two other common law forms of concurrent ownership that you will likely not study in your Property course. The first of these is coparceny, which was an alternative to male ownership under the common law rules of primogeniture when an individual fathered only daughters, and the second is the tenancy in partnership. Coparceny is of no consequence at all today given the rejection of the law of primogeniture, and the common law rules relating to tenancy in partnership have largely been subsumed by state statutes, including the Uniform Partnership Act. Those statutes will be part of one of your future courses relating to business entities.

unlike the tenancy in common, each co-owner has survivorship rights. For example, suppose that O transfers property "to A, B, and C as joint tenants with right of survivorship." Each of the three owners has a 33.33% undivided interest in the whole parcel, along with survivorship rights. If A dies, then B and C automatically become owners of A's former portion, and thereafter each has a 50% undivided interest in the property. In turn, when B dies, then C automatically becomes the sole owner of the property. This right of survivorship interest is not an interest that is devisable or descendible.

There is sometimes confusion relating to nomenclature regarding the joint tenancy with right of survivorship. For example, two or more co-owners of property might be called "joint owners." Standing alone, this may well refer only to co-ownership as tenants in common. Typically, a drafter must provide a clear indication that a conveyance or bequest was intended to carry with it survivorship rights. At common law, in large part due to a desire to keep parcels of land intact, the favored construction was for a joint tenancy with right of survivorship. In contrast, under modern law the opposite is true. Any presumption in favor of survivorship rights has largely been discarded. Thus, the careful drafter will want to include language such as "to A and B as joint tenants with rights of survivorship" or "to A and B as joint tenants, and not as tenants in common." A simple grant "to A and B as joint owners" or "to A and B jointly" might not be construed to include survivorship rights. In fact, some states have statutes that require a provision that expressly identifies the inclusion of survivorship rights to create this type of tenancy.

Under common law rules, and in many states today, a joint tenancy with right of survivorship will be created only when the four unities of time, title, interest, and possession are present. (A helpful mnemonic to remember these unities is TTIP — representing the first letter of each unity.) Accordingly, upon creation, all of the joint tenants must have acquired their interests at the same time; they must have received their title via the same instrument (such as a single deed or will); they must have received the same percentage share in the estate, both as to relative size and duration; and they must have been granted equal rights to possession and use of the whole. Note, however, that after the joint tenancy is created, one of the joint owners can choose to allow exclusive possession by the other joint owner(s).

A joint tenant may sever the joint tenancy with right of survivorship in whole or in part by transferring his or her interest. For example, suppose that A and B own Blackacre as joint tenants with right of survivorship. If A sells her interest to C, that would sever the joint tenancy with right of survivorship. Thereafter, C and B would own Blackacre as tenants in common. However, suppose that X, Y, and Z acquire Purpleacre as joint tenants with right of survivorship. Thereafter, X gives his interest to his daughter D. After that conveyance, D would own a 1/3 undivided interest in Purpleacre as a tenant in common with Y and Z. There would only be a partial severance of the joint tenancy, however, as Y and Z would continue to hold their 1/3 interests as to each other in joint tenancy with right of survivorship. Accordingly, if Z should then die, Y would automatically become the owner of a 2/3 undivided interest in Purpleacre and hold title as a tenant in common with D.

A *tenancy by the entirety* is similar to a joint tenancy with right of survivorship, but can generally only be created between a husband and a wife. In effect, this form of property ownership adds a fifth unity — marriage — to the four required for a joint tenancy with right of survivorship. Unlike the joint tenancy with right of survivorship, however, the tenancy by the entirety cannot be unilaterally severed by one of the spouse co-owners. Instead, the tenancy by the entirety will only come to an end upon death of one of the spouses, divorce, or by agreement of the two spouses. The tenancy by the entirety is recognized by fewer than half the states. Because it involves a form of property ownership involved with marital interests, an example problem is included in Chapter 5 pertaining to Marital Interests in Property, rather than in this chapter.

Not surprisingly, when co-owners have fractional ownership interests in real property, but also possess rights as to the undivided whole of the property, conflicts can arise. These are often addressed by agreements between the co-owners, but more significant disputes can ensue. These might result in one co-owner buying out the other co-owner(s). Alternatively, a tenant in common or a joint tenant with right of survivorship has an absolute right to file an action for partition in the courts. The judge typically has discretion to order a partition by sale (in which the property is sold and the proceeds are divided) or a partition in kind (an order providing an actual division of the property between the former co-owners). Although some courts tend to favor a partition in kind, most courts generally favor a partition by sale, particularly when the parcel is not readily divisible into fractional portions. The prospect of a judicially directed partition by sale will often cause parties to negotiate their own resolution or division of the property.

Other issues can arise between co-owners. If the property is leased out to third persons, any rents are ordinarily to be divided proportionately among the co-owners. If one of the co-owners is in exclusive possession, however, normally the other co-owners cannot obtain rent from the party in possession. This is the case because each owner has an undivided interest in the whole property. The co-tenant out of possession can obtain a share of rental value from the occupying co-tenant if the co-tenant in possession *ousts* the non-occupying co-tenant. An *ouster* can occur when the non-occupying co-tenant makes a demand for entry and is refused. This rule can obviously create disharmony between the co-owners.

EXERCISE 3-1

GENERAL DESCRIPTION OF EXERCISE: Addressing legal questions that arise between co-owners of property following the death of a spouse/parent.

SKILLS INVOLVED: Fact analysis and development, statutory research and construction, creative problem solving, preparation for and participation in negotiations and mediation, drafting of agreements.

PARTICIPANTS NEEDED: Tasks 1, 3, and 4 are individual projects, and Tasks 2 and 5 are collaborative and require four students each.

ESTIMATED TIME REQUIRED:

Task 1: 30 minutes

Task 2: 30 minutes to prepare and 30-45 minutes to meet and negotiate

Task 3: One hour — 30 minutes to analyze and 30 minutes to prepare a letter

Task 4: One hour — 30 minutes to analyze and 30 minutes to prepare a memorandum

Task 5: 30 minutes to prepare and 45-60 minutes to mediate

LEVEL OF DIFFICULTY (1-5):

ROLES IN EXERCISE: You are acting as a lawyer for the parties as identified in the various tasks. In one task you might be designated to serve as a mediator.

THE EXERCISE: 3-1

Wilma recently died at the age of 76. Her first husband, Harry, had pre-deceased her ten years earlier. Wilma and Harry had two children, Alice and Bob, who are 46 and 48 years old, respectively. After Harry's death, Wilma became the sole owner of Greenacre, a parcel of land consisting of 100 acres. Her home is located in the northwest corner of Greenacre. Most of the land is under cultivation. There are 80 acres of fields that are typically planted with crops of wheat or cotton, and there are also 10 acres of grapevines that produce grapes for making wine. Wilma never raised livestock on the property, but she did have a number of chickens, and a henhouse is located on the property. There has typically only been enough egg production for home consumption, and Wilma at times gave away excess eggs to the county's food bank. (She would also occasionally kill a rooster for Sunday dinner.) There are also two water wells on the east side of the property near the easternmost boundary. Water from these wells is used for crop irrigation as needed. In addition, water pipes run across the property from the wells to supply water to the home.

Five years ago, Wilma got re-married to Homer. Homer lived in a nearby town and was a widower with one son, Carl. After he and Wilma married, Homer sold his house in town and moved in with Wilma on Greenacre. Although Homer and Wilma were very much in love, Alice and Bob were wary of Homer and never got along well with him. Alice and Bob continued to live nearby, but Carl was a doctor who lived in a large city in another state. Wilma never got around to preparing a will, and she died intestate. She is survived by Homer, Alice, and Bob. Aside from Greenacre, she owned no other real property.

TASK 1: Assume that you represent Homer. Alice and Bob have demanded that he vacate Greenacre at once. He has come to see you to ask about his rights, if any, to Greenacre. (There is also some personal property, a shared bank account, and some mutual funds, but at present Homer is primarily interested in your assessment regarding Greenacre.) You are to assume that Greenacre is located in a state that has adopted a property distribution statute that is identical to provisions under Illinois law. A link to the relevant provisions is included on the **LexisNexis Webcourse** for this chapter. In addition, you are to assume that the state's probate code includes additional statutes relating to homestead rights, which are also available by a link that is included on the **LexisNexis Webcourse** for this chapter. Read and analyze the linked statutes and write a brief memorandum summarizing Homer's likely rights, if any, in Greenacre.

TASK 2: Assume that your research for Task 1 reveals that Homer, Alice, and Bob are now co-owners of Greenacre. In addition, Homer has certain homestead rights as determined through your analysis in Task 1. Heated disputes have arisen between Alice and Bob, Wilma's surviving children, and Homer, Wilma's widower. Alice and Bob are adamant that their late mother had assured them repeatedly during her lifetime that Greenacre would be theirs upon her death. Homer recognizes that Alice and Bob have some interest in Greenacre, but he views Greenacre as his home. He is also of the view that Alice and Bob do not really want Greenacre, but have always resented that he married their mother after their father had passed away. In fact, on more than one occasion, he has heard each of them mutter the term, "gold-digger," in his presence.

Alice and Bob have now retained an attorney, and Homer also has an attorney. This task is a negotiation exercise. Located on the **LexisNexis Webcourse** for this part of the exercise are short videos of client interviews between Alice and Bob and their counsel and between Homer and his counsel. Your professor will assign you to work in pairs and for each pair to represent either Alice and Bob or Homer. After reviewing and considering the respective video featuring your client(s), you are to (1) develop your plan and strategy for a negotiation session with counsel for the opposing side; (2) engage in a negotiation with the pair of students who are representing the opposing side — your professor will identify the match-ups for the negotiation sessions; and (3) draft a memorandum of agreement if you are able to reach a settlement during the negotiation session.

TASK 3: For purposes of this task, you are to assume that Alice and Bob were able to negotiate a deal in which they bought out Homer's interest in Greenacre. Following Homer's transfer of his interest, Alice and Bob now each own an undivided one-half interest in Greenacre as tenants in common. Alice is a family physician whose medical practice is in Smallville, a small town located approximately 25 miles from Greenacre. Alice also has a home in Smallville with her husband, Andy, and three children. She has no interest in moving from her home and does not wish to reside at Greenacre. Bob, on the other hand, is a farmer. He and his wife, Betty, own a small home that is located on their 60-acre farm, Redacre. Greenacre is less than five miles away from Redacre. Because the house and farming operations at Greenacre are larger and more attractive to Bob and Betty, they have decided to move to Greenacre and to lease out Redacre. (Bob and Betty's two children are grown and have left home.) Alice has no objections. She does not want to leave Smallville and is happy that her brother and sister-in-law will be living at the family place. In fact, she had been worried that she and Bob might have to lease out Greenacre to some stranger.

Assume that before moving to Greenacre, Bob has contacted you to seek your advice. He is uncertain regarding his rights and obligations with respect to Greenacre. He has told you that there are several bank loans outstanding with the First State Bank of Smallville, which necessitates a monthly mortgage payment. (Greenacre was pledged as collateral for these loans.) Bob wants to know whether Alice has any obligation to share in these mortgage payments. He would also like to know whether Alice should pay her share of the real estate taxes, homeowners' insurance, crop insurance, and monthly utility bills. Bob and Betty also plan to take out a $60,000 home improvement loan. They are going to renovate and update the kitchen and both bathrooms of the house on Greenacre. Because these improvements will add to the overall value of Greenacre, Bob believes that Alice should shoulder a share of the costs. Finally, Bob has asked about the co-owners' respective duties concerning the crops. Typically, the wheat or cotton crops raised on the 80-acre field have been sold after harvest. The annual grape production from the 10 acres of grapevines has been subject to a long-term supply contract with a nearby winery located within the county. Bob wants to know whether he must split the income from these crops with Alice, and whether Alice must share in the cultivation costs. (These costs include routine items such as seed, fertilizer, pesticide, and labor — both Bob's own efforts, as well as part-time hired help.) Your task is to review the links provided on the **LexisNexis Webcourse** for this part of the exercise and to prepare a client letter to Bob that sets out your analysis of these items. After you have prepared your letter, exchange it with the letter created by one of your classmates. Compare whether you included the same information.

TASK 4: Assume that five years have passed since Bob and Betty moved to Greenacre. Several months ago, Bob and Betty decided to leave Greenacre and move back to Redacre. Bob and Alice had been approached by a large corporate farming operation, Farmco, which made inquiries about leasing Greenacre. Alice strongly objected to any deal, but Bob nonetheless entered into a five-year lease with Farmco by which Farmco has leased both the house and the 80 acres of fields in which wheat and cotton have been raised over the years. The lease did not include the 10 acres of grapevines, which Bob plans to continue cultivating (although he and Betty will now be living on Redacre). Farmco plans to allow their farm foreman and his family to live in the house on Greenacre. In addition, they plan to convert the 80-acre farming operation from crop cultivation to a hog-raising operation. Alice is very unhappy about these developments, and she has consulted you for advice. After reviewing the links located on the **LexisNexis Webcourse** for this part of the exercise, and in preparation for an upcoming client meeting with Alice, prepare a brief memorandum that sets out your views of Alice's options at this point.

TASK 5: Rather than the facts set forth in Task 4 above, assume that after Alice objected to the possible lease with Farmco, Bob instead leased 90 acres of Greenacre to Ray for a three-year term. The acreage included both the 80 acres of wheat/cotton fields and the 10 acres of grapevines. Alice did not join in the lease, but did not have the same type of concerns or objections to Ray as she did with regard to Farmco. Ray did not live on the property, but lived on his own farm just down the road. Ray continued the farming operations in a manner similar to those followed in years past (cultivation of crops on the 80 acres of fields and grape production on the 10 acres of grapevines). Ray paid rent on a monthly basis to Bob, and in turn, Bob sent a check for half of the total rent to Alice each month. After Bob and Betty moved back to Redacre, their son, Sam, moved into the house on Greenacre. Sam had been a college student at Big State University, but his grades were very poor. Accordingly, he returned home and began attending classes at Small County Community College, which is located ten miles from Greenacre.

Two years went by quite smoothly. Unfortunately, however, Alice just learned that Andy, her husband of 26 years, has been having an affair with Alice's office manager. Given this development, Alice has decided to separate from her husband and file for divorce. She has told both Bob and Ray that she wants to move into her mother's old house on Greenacre as soon as possible, and that she will thereafter commute from Greenacre into Smallville to her medical office. She recognizes that Ray still has a year remaining on his lease from Bob, but she can no longer remain in the house in Smallville. Assume that Alice, Bob, and Ray have now each retained counsel. They have authorized their lawyers to meet with a mediator at the Smallville Dispute Resolution Center to discuss a possible resolution of the current situation. Your professor will assign you to represent Alice, Bob, or Ray, or to serve as the mediator. Located on the **LexisNexis Webcourse** for this part of the exercise are short videos of client interviews between Alice, Bob, Ray, and their respective counsel. There is also a link to information for those of you who are designated by your professor to serve as the mediator. After reviewing and considering the linked material for your role, you are to (1) develop your plan and strategy for the mediation session; (2) participate in a mediation — your professor will identify the match-ups for these sessions; and (3) draft a memorandum of agreement if you are able to reach a settlement during the mediation.

EXERCISE 3-2

GENERAL DESCRIPTION OF EXERCISE: Addressing legal questions that arise between co-owners of property who hold title as joint tenants with right of survivorship

SKILLS INVOLVED: Fact and statutory analysis, creative problem solving, preparation for a client meeting, use of forms to prepare a deed

PARTICIPANTS NEEDED: Tasks 1 and 3 are individual projects, and Task 2 is collaborative and requires two students.

ESTIMATED TIME REQUIRED:

Task 1: 30 minutes

Task 2: One hour — 30 minutes to prepare and 30 minutes to draft a deed

Task 3: One hour — 30 minutes to analyze and 30 minutes to prepare a letter

LEVEL OF DIFFICULTY (1-5):

ROLES IN EXERCISE: You are acting as a lawyer for the parties as identified in the various tasks.

THE EXERCISE: 3-2

Maude, an 82-year-old widow, recently died. She was survived by her three children: Ann (age 56), Bill (age 54), and Carl (age 51). Among Maude's effects, the family has located a holographic will that Maude had apparently written out at some point with the help of a form book that she apparently purchased at Big National Bookstore. You have determined that, while somewhat unorthodox in its phrasing, the will is valid under your state's law. Of particular interest for this exercise, the handwritten will included the following provision:

> *I leave my ranch to my three wonderful children, and they are to own it in equal shares as joint tenants with right of survivorship.*

TASK 1:   It is undisputed that the ranch referred to in Maude's will is a 600-acre parcel of ranch land known as Sageacre. A small house, two barns, and several stock pens are located on the property, and the ranch has primarily been used for sheep and goat grazing. In fact, Maude participated in shearing activities until her 81st birthday! For purposes of this task, assume that Maude's daughter, Ann, is a very wealthy author who lives in Big City. She has told Carl, your client, that she has no interest in anything to do with Sageacre. She misses her mother, but has no desire to own ranch property. Her children grew up in Big City, as well, and neither of them has any interest in ever possessing an interest in Sageacre. Carl has told you that Ann has had a long-time feud with their brother Bill. Apparently, more than 20 years ago, Bill called Ann's first novel (an enormously successful lawyer fiction mystery), a "pile of worthless drivel with a plot that could have been crafted by a none-too-bright third grader." Given this feud, Ann has apparently called Carl and offered to give Carl her interest in Sageacre. Carl has asked you for advice. He wants to know "whether this is legal." In addition, he has asked you to let him know what the parties' rights would be if this transfer is accomplished. Your task is to review the introductory materials to this chapter and the linked case on the **LexisNexis Webcourse** for this Task, and then prepare a brief memorandum that assesses Carl's queries.

TASK 2:   Using the sample form documents referenced in the **LexisNexis Webcourse** for this part of the exercise, draft a deed of gift from Ann to Carl that transfers her interest in Sageacre. Their full names are Ann Johnson Smithers and Carl D. Johnson. You need not worry about the precise metes and bounds description of Sageacre for purposes of your deed. After you have drafted your deed, meet with a classmate to exchange and compare deeds. Discuss any differences that you find.

TASK 3:   Assume that two years after Ann's gift of her interest in Sageacre to Carl, Bill and Carl entered into a five-year lease of Sageacre to Tom. Under the lease, Tom agreed to pay rent to Bill and Carl in proportion to their ownership interests. Tom has now been in exclusive possession of the property for a year. Assume also that Bill has recently had some financial problems. He has determined that he needs to borrow $80,000 to avoid possible bankruptcy. The local banks have viewed him as a poor credit risk and have declined to loan him money. Thereafter, he met with his father-in-law, Frank, and asked Frank to loan him the money. Bill has offered to pledge his interest in Sageacre as collateral for the loan. Frank is considering whether to do so, but has asked you for advice. Frank is planning to drop by your office later this week to discuss the possible transaction with you. Read the linked materials in the **LexisNexis Webcourse** for this exercise and prepare a list of talking points for your client meeting. (For purposes of this problem, you are to assume that you are not the same lawyer who previously represented Carl.)

Chapter 4

CO-OWNERSHIP OF PROPERTY: PERSONAL PROPERTY — ACCOUNTS AT FINANCIAL INSTITUTIONS

INTRODUCTION

In Chapter 3 we discussed and you considered problems relating to the co-ownership of real property.[1] Two or more persons can also share ownership of personal property. Let us list a few examples. First, suppose that upon O's death, she leaves all her property by will "to my children A and B." Today, A and B would likely each inherit an undivided one-half interest in all of the real and personal property as tenants in common. As for the personal property, cash assets can be readily divided, but issues might arise as to the remaining personal property. Another example is the acquisition of personal property by a married couple in a community property state. In those states, property acquired by either spouse after marriage is presumptively community property (and owned one-half each). Finally, it is very common for more than one person to have an ownership interest in an account at a financial institution. This chapter will focus on several exercises involving multi-party accounts.

Multi-party accounts are generally creatures of contract law, but there are overlapping property law concepts at work, as well. Financial institutions such as banks, savings and loan associations, and credit unions enter into contractual arrangements with their customers. Typical accounts include checking accounts, savings accounts, and certificates of deposit. Comparable agreements also cover the relationships between financial institutions and customers as to safety deposit boxes. When more than one customer wants to open a joint or other multi-party form of account, the contractual arrangement between the financial institution and the customers will often be controlling, but governing state law is also pertinent. These account agreements and relevant state law relate both to the account holders' interests in the account during lifetime, but also with regard to the disposition of funds on deposit in these accounts upon the death of one of the depositors. Depositors routinely open multiple-party accounts at financial institutions without consulting counsel. The new accounts officer at the financial institution might try to explain the differing forms of accounts, but typically this person has no legal training. Whether

---

[1] In Chapter 3, we also discussed the three types of common law co-ownership of property that remain important today: (1) the tenancy in common, (2) the joint tenancy with right of survivorship, and (3) the tenancy by the entirety. That summary will not be repeated here. Additional marital property issues will be addressed in Chapter 5.

the advice given is accurate or in the best interests of the particular depositors can be in question.

There are four general types of multiple-party accounts: (1) the joint account, (2) the convenience or agency account, (3) the payable on death account, and (4) the trust account, sometimes known as the Totten trust.

A *joint account* is a form of multi-party account in which two or more persons deposit funds that are payable upon the request of any of the parties. Typically, during the parties' lifetimes, the ownership of the funds in the joint account belongs to the parties in proportion to the amount of net contributions made by each party. Unless there is clear evidence of intent or an agreement to the contrary, note that there is no transfer of ownership rights to any other co-depositor. An individual depositor's ownership share would be calculated by adding all of that party's deposits, subtracting any withdrawals, and adding a pro rata share of any interest or dividends. Accordingly, the opening of a joint account does not have the same consequences as the creation of a joint tenancy with right of survivorship by which a contributing joint tenant would be deemed to have made a gift to the non-contributing joint tenant.[2]

Although the ownership of the funds in the joint account is proportionate to the net contributions that each party has made, any of the joint owners has the right to withdraw any or all of the funds in the account. Obviously, there should be some degree of trust between the parties to a joint account! The financial institution typically will not be liable for paying out funds in a manner that is contrary to the parties' percentage ownership rights unless there has been some written notice to the contrary in advance of the withdrawal. If one of the parties to a joint account withdraws more than his or her proportionate share, the other party or parties to the account may have a claim for conversion as to the excess funds that were withdrawn. The claim would be against the "over-withdrawing" party, or if that person has died, against that party's estate.

When one of the parties to a joint account dies, if the account does not include a survivorship feature, the deceased party's net contributions to the account pass through that person's estate to the party's heirs or will beneficiaries. If, however, the joint account includes a survivorship feature, then the remaining joint parties become the owners of the deceased joint owners' contributions. Some jurisdictions presume that joint accounts include a survivorship feature. In other states, there is no such presumption, and the parties must expressly create survivorship rights through the account agreement with the financial institution. The account contract could also include language that varies a particular state's presumption on this issue. Finally, some courts are very restrictive in allowing extrinsic evidence to be introduced that might vary the terms set forth in the account contract.

A *convenience* or *agency account* is an account by which the owner of the account or joint owners in a joint account permit another party to have access to the account to assist the depositor(s) in handling transactions. It is a primitive form of agency

---

[2] In a community property jurisdiction, deposits of community funds by either or both spouses in a joint account would remain as community funds. Community property issues will be discussed, *infra*, in Chapter 5.

relationship, and is much less sweeping than a power of attorney. It is often employed in the event of disability or infirmity by the owner or owners of the account. All funds in the account remain the property of the actual account owner or owners (i.e., the depositors), even though the convenience signer has the right to withdraw funds on behalf of the owner(s). The convenience signer has no rights of survivorship in the account funds in the event of death of the account owner.

A *payable on death (P.O.D.) account* is a form of account in which the deposited funds become payable to a designated person or persons — the P.O.D. payee(s) — upon the death of all the original depositors. The P.O.D. payees have no ownership interest in the account funds during the lifetime(s) of the depositor(s). The actual depositors have the unrestricted right to make withdrawals at any time (even of all the funds). This type of account is of fairly recent origin. It is a creature of the deposit contract with the financial institution. At one time there was reluctance by courts to recognize this form of account because the utilization of a contract to transfer funds at death sidesteps the formalities of transferring property via a will. Today, however, most states recognize the use of P.O.D. accounts and designations.

A *trust account* is an account in which a named beneficiary or beneficiaries receive the account balance after the death of all trustees to the account. Under such an account, funds are held in a form such as, "Depositor, in trust for Beneficiary." The trust account operates similarly to the P.O.D. account. That is, after the deaths of all trustees (i.e., the depositors), the designated, surviving trustees become owners of the account. The beneficiaries have no ability to withdraw any funds from the account while any of the trustees (i.e., the depositors) is alive. This type of account is sometimes known as a *Totten trust*, based on the New York case of *In re Totten*, 179 N.Y. 112, 71 N.E. 748 (1904), in which the court recognized the validity of this form of revocable trust.

EXERCISE 4-1

GENERAL DESCRIPTION OF EXERCISE: Addressing legal questions that arise involving depositors in multiple-party accounts at financial institutions.

SKILLS INVOLVED: Fact analysis and development, statutory research and construction, statutory drafting, case analysis, creative problem solving, client counseling, drafting of documents.

PARTICIPANTS NEEDED: Tasks 1, 2, and 5 are individual projects, and Tasks 3 and 4 are collaborative and require two students each.

ESTIMATED TIME REQUIRED:

Task 1: 45 minutes

Task 2: 30 minutes

Task 3: One hour — 30 minutes to analyze and 30 minutes to prepare draft legislation

Task 4: One hour — 30 minutes to analyze and 30 minutes to prepare relevant contract provisions

Task 5: One hour & 15 minutes — 45 minutes to analyze and 30 minutes to draft language for inclusion in a letter to a financial institution

LEVEL OF DIFFICULTY (1-5):

ROLES IN EXERCISE: You are acting as a lawyer for a party as identified in the various tasks.

THE EXERCISE: 4-1

Your client, Wanda Smith, called earlier in the day. She is a 68-year old widow whose husband, Howell, died about six months ago. Wanda has three adult children: Andy, Betty, and Cindy. Cindy lives across town from Wanda, but Andy and Betty reside in other states. Wanda has told you that she would like to put Cindy's name on all of her bank accounts. She related that she had knee replacement surgery last year, and was not able to get to the bank on her own for about a month. With Howell now deceased, she is anxious that if she becomes home-bound in the future, she could not get to the bank on her own. Wanda also informed you that her good friend Frieda had told her the following over coffee last week: "I was worried about the same thing, so I made Biff, my eldest son, a joint owner of my bank accounts to help me out as needed." Wanda plans to come by your office for a meeting about her options early next week.

TASK 1:   Assume that you practice in the state of Minnetoba. Review several pertinent Minnetoba statutory provisions to explore Wanda's options prior to the client meeting. These statutes are set forth in the e-materials on the **LexisNexis Webcourse** that accompany this chapter for Task 1. After reviewing the statutory excerpts, generate a list of several pros and cons about the different account options identified in these statutes to prepare for and facilitate the client counseling session with Wanda. Exchange your list with that of a classmate and discuss the similarities or differences between your respective lists.

TASK 2:   Assume that you are now meeting with your client, Wanda Smith, in your office. First, review the client interview video that is available on the **LexisNexis Webcourse** for this chapter. Then, reconsider the Minnetoba statutes and the list of pros and cons that you generated for Task 1. Given your client's wishes, analyze whether she should consider a convenience account, a multi-party account with right of survivorship, or a multi-party account without right of survivorship. In addition, should you advise your client as to any risks in adding Cindy as a co-owner or as a convenience signer? Consider, also, whether you should advise Wanda about the option of including a payable-on-death provision for the accounts.

TASK 3:   For purposes of this task, assume that you are a staff attorney who works for the Minnetoba Association of Retired Persons (MARP). MARP describes itself as a voluntary membership organization formed to provide leadership, value, and desirable social change for Minnetobans of age 55 and over through advocacy and service. About fifteen years ago, MARP had been a leading force in persuading the Minnetoba legislature to enact the current Minnetoba legislation that authorizes convenience accounts. The MARP legislative affairs committee has now identified another common problem. In our aging society, many baby boomers are currently living much longer lives than in generations past. Often, both spouses are living longer. In many households, however, two elderly spouses can find themselves either disabled or otherwise unable to regularly take care of routine transactions such as banking. Although current Minnetoba law authorizes the creation of convenience accounts with a person designated as a convenience signer, it is unclear whether the statutes authorize adding a convenience signer to some other form of multi-party account. For example, two elderly spouses may own their bank accounts as joint tenants with right of survivorship, but also desire identifying a third person, typically a responsible adult son or daughter, to be designated as a convenience signer. Your task is to draft appropriate language for inclusion in legislation to amend Minnetoba law to authorize the utilization of a convenience signer for any form of multi-party account. To accomplish this task, work with another student. Then, before proceeding, review the Minnetoba statutes that are set forth on the **LexisNexis Webcourse** for this chapter for Task 1. In addition, the **LexisNexis Webcourse** for Task 3 includes links to other sources that will be of use to you in your drafting efforts.

TASK 4:   For purposes of this task, you are to assume that legislation along the lines described in Task 3 has now been enacted by the Minnetoba legislature. That is, financial institutions may now permit the establishment of convenience accounts, but also can authorize the addition of a convenience signer to any new or existing account. Accordingly, financial institutions may authorize the party or parties to single-party or multi-party accounts to designate a convenience signer for the accounts. Assume that your law firm does a significant amount of work for Minnetoba State Bank (MSB). MSB is the largest state bank in Minnetoba and has branches in both large and small cities around the state. MSB has long authorized multi-party accounts including joint accounts with rights of survivorship and accounts with P.O.D. designations. However, MSB has never previously authorized the establishment of convenience accounts. Recently, a group known as the Minnetoba Association of Retired Persons (MARP) has been complaining to your client's top officials about this lack of access to convenience account options. In fact, MARP has been threatening to urge its members to stop banking with MSB and to move their accounts to financial institutions which they claim are "more receptive and friendly to aging customers." Accordingly, MSB has asked your firm to provide them with some language that they can add to their standard account agreement forms to authorize convenience accounts and convenience signers for other accounts. Your tasks are (1) to review the sample agreement forms and related materials that are available in the **LexisNexis Webcourse** for this chapter, and (2) to work with a classmate to draft language that will accomplish MSB's desired result.

TASK 5:   Rather than the joint account issues addressed in the foregoing problems, this task will focus on joint interests in a safe (or "safety") deposit box at a financial institution. Typically, the use of a safe deposit box is not viewed as an account at the financial institution. Instead, the financial institution and the customer or customers enter into a leasing arrangement regarding the safe deposit box. Issues can arise with regard to the ownership of the contents of the safe deposit box.

For purposes of this task, let us return to the general facts provided for Tasks 1 and 2, which involved Wanda Smith and her financial affairs. You will recall that Wanda recently became a widow and has three adult children: Andy, Betty, and Cindy. Only Cindy, however, lives in the same town and state as does Wanda. Assume further that during your initial client meeting with Wanda, you learned that Wanda has a safe deposit box at the Tunatown Teachers' Credit Union (in Tunatown, Minnetoba). Wanda also informed you that about a week before her meeting with you, she and her daughter Cindy had visited the credit union. At that time, she asked the appropriate staff person at the credit union to add Cindy's name to the signature card for the safe deposit box to allow Cindy to have access. The credit union official promptly located the card in a small file case near the safe deposit boxes, scratched out the name of Howell Smith (Wanda's late husband), and typed in Cindy's full name on the card. Cindy then placed her signature on the card next to her typed name. The card was then copied, and the credit union officer provided copies to both Wanda and Cindy. Wanda provided you with her copy during your client meeting. The following was printed at the top of the signature card: "Safe Deposit Box Lease Agreement." In addition to the two names and signatures for Wanda and Cindy, and the scratched-out name and signature for Howell, among the pre-printed language was the following:

Joint Lease

In the event that there are two or more lessees, the lessees are deemed to be joint tenants under the lease, and any and all property that is placed in the safe deposit box at any time is deemed to be their joint property, and upon the death of a lessee said property passes to the survivor(s).

After your discussion with Wanda about her various accounts and the safe deposit box, assume that she makes it clear that she wants Cindy only to have access to the safe deposit box. She does not desire that Cindy have any present ownership interests in the contents of the box. Wanda's primary worry is about access to the box in the event that she is too ill or disabled to get to the credit union on her own. Your task is to review and analyze the cases and annotations that are identified in the **LexisNexis Webcourse** that accompany this chapter for Task 5. After doing so, determine whether you should write a letter to the credit union on behalf of your client suggesting other operative language for the safe deposit box agreement. If so, draft language that you would like the credit union to substitute for the "Joint Lease" language quoted above. After doing so, exchange drafts with another student and compare approaches.

Chapter 5

MARITAL INTERESTS IN PROPERTY

INTRODUCTION

It should come as no surprise that the marital relationship impacts many different areas of property law. For example, for most couples, the marital home will likely represent both the largest asset and the most substantial debt of both spouses' lives. The typical first-year Property course will just scratch the surface of many of the issues that are covered in much more detail in upper division courses such as Family Law, Marital Property, Wills & Trusts, Estate Planning, and more. This chapter will focus on practical problems that relate to key topic areas that are typically included in first-year Property casebooks.

The vast majority of states adhere to the *separate property* system. This system derived from the English common law property system, albeit modified significantly by statutes over time. The roots of this system were dominated by gender bias in favor of husbands. At common law, upon marriage, the wife was to receive the husband's protection or *cover*, but gave up her rights to most real and personal property. The husband thus controlled the marital property during marriage. If a wife outlived her husband, at common law, she held a *dower* interest which provided her merely with a life estate in 1/3 of all freehold land owned by her husband and inheritable by their issue. Today, dower is recognized in only a few states, and legislative enactments in all common law property states in the 1800s known as Married Women's Property Acts gave the wife the same property rights as a single woman (or single or married man) to be able to own, dispose, and manage her property.

In separate property jurisdictions today, during the marriage each spouse separately owns and controls the property that has been acquired by that spouse. Accordingly, the wife's and husband's earnings during marriage are each spouse's respective separate property, as are items of property that are purchased with those separate earnings. A creditor of one spouse cannot ordinarily reach the separate assets of the other spouse absent some form of agreement relating to joint ownership by the spouses. For example, the spouses incur a joint debt or agree to hold property as joint owners.

Upon a divorce, statutes in most separate property jurisdictions change the foregoing approach and call for the court to make an *equitable distribution* of the property accumulated during marriage. The fact that property might have otherwise been the wife's or husband's separate property is no longer relevant, and the court is to endeavor to make a fair and just division of the property. Some states extend the requirement for an equitable distribution of the marital property to all property —

even that owned by either spouse prior to the marriage — while other states limit the requirement for an equitable distribution to that property acquired during the marriage. In determining the property division, the court may consider a broad array of factors ranging from need, income(s), debts, marketable skills, prior lifestyle, age, health, and — in some states — fault.

Separate property states have also enacted statutes to protect a surviving spouse upon the death of the other spouse. These statutes make available to the surviving spouse the opportunity for a *forced share* or *elective share* of the deceased spouse's estate. For example, if the deceased spouse left a substantial portion of that spouse's estate to someone other than the surviving spouse, then the surviving spouse could elect to take either the amount left to the survivor under the will or, alternatively, claim the designated statutory share per the statute. This statutory portion varies by state, but typically is either a one-half or one-third share. The Uniform Probate Code, which has been adopted by a number of states, includes a laddered share approach in which surviving spouses in shorter-term marriages are entitled to elect a smaller percentage of the estate than surviving spouses in longer-term marriages. In the event that there is no will, the state's intestacy statute will control. Depending on the state, these statutes typically provide the surviving spouse with either all of the deceased spouse's separate property or create a division of the decedent's property between the surviving spouse and the children of the deceased spouse. Keep in mind, however, that wills, elective share statutes, and intestacy statutes generally only control probate assets, and not other forms of property ownership such as property held as joint tenants with right of survivorship or as tenants by the entirety, or contractual benefits such as life insurance proceeds.

Other states have adopted the *community property* system. Largely influenced by Spanish or French civil law, eight southwestern and western states have long had a system of community property (Louisiana, Texas, New Mexico, Arizona, California, Idaho, Nevada, and Washington). Wisconsin has adopted the approach more recently by statute, and Alaska law allows spouses to elect to hold their property as community. Based on the concept that the two spouses contribute equally in a marriage, the underlying premise in community property states is that all earnings during marriage by either spouse are owned equally by both spouses, as are assets then purchased with those earnings. Property owned before marriage by either spouse remains separate property, and the same is true of property acquired during marriage by gift or inheritance. In some of the community property states, any income from separate property is viewed as community property, but in the other community property states, that income remains separate property. There is also a presumption that all property owned by either spouse is community property. Accordingly, a spouse who asserts that certain assets are separate property has the burden of tracing the separate character of the property.

If spouses divorce in a community property state, some of the states require an equal distribution of the community estate. Others, like separate property law states, task the courts with making an *equitable distribution* of the community property (although either spouse's separate property, if any, is typically not subject to such an equitable distribution). Upon death, each spouse has the power to distribute by will all of that spouse's separate property and one-half of the community estate. Because of this equal distribution of the community estate upon the death of either spouse, community property states generally do not have forced or elective share statutes.

Issues can arise when property was first purchased when the spouses were still single, but payments continue to be made after their marriage. Several of the community property states apply an *inception of title* approach to this type of situation, and treat the property as remaining separate when initially acquired prior to the marriage. Of course, payments made after the marriage will presumptively come from community funds, and the states apply various approaches to recognizing the community contribution to the enhancement of such a separate asset. Those community property states that do not adhere to the inception of title rule, instead apply a *pro rata apportionment approach*. Under this latter approach, a percentage of the asset's value consistent with the amount of payments made before marriage will be treated as separate property, and the percentage of the asset's value consistent with payments made during the marriage will be regarded as community property. Thus, a single item of property can be partially separate and community in nature.

In modern society, many couples obviously move from state to state. Challenging legal and practical issues can arise when married couples move either from a separate property jurisdiction to a community property state or the reverse, or even from a community property state that follows the pro rata apportionment rule to an inception of title state. Typically, the nature of ownership of an asset will be determined under the laws of the state in which the couple was living at the time the asset was acquired. Moreover, the nature of that ownership will not change when the couple moves to a new state absent some agreement between the spouses. When spouses move from a separate property jurisdiction to a community property state, the new state will employ the concept of *quasi-community property* to treat any separate property that was earned by either of the spouses in the separate property state as if it had been earned in a community property state. That is, the earnings will be deemed to be community in nature for certain purposes. Those purposes vary, however, among community property states. Some of the states apply the concept of quasi-community property in cases of either divorce or death. Other states limit the application of quasi-community property rules solely to divorces or solely to the death of one of the spouses.

In addition to some of the variations between separate property and community property jurisdictions described above, a significant difference between the two types of property systems is the effect of deed recitals regarding ownership rights of the spouses. The general rule in a separate property law state is that the manner in which title is taken will determine ownership. The same rule applies to personal property such as stock. There is no focus on the timing of the acquisition (whether before or after marriage) or the nature of the funds used. If title is taken in just one spouse's name, it is considered to be that spouse's property. If title is taken in both spouses names, it is their jointly owned property, and will likely be further designated as being held as a tenancy in common, a joint tenancy with right of survivorship, or in some states as a tenancy by the entirety. By way of contrast, for assets acquired during the marriage in community property states, the general rule is just the opposite; that is, the manner in which title to property is taken and reflected, for example, on a deed, is not controlling. There is a presumption that all property acquired during marriage is community in nature. Thus, the deed recitals are not controlling, and the nature of ownership is dictated by the timing of the acquisition (whether before or following the wedding date) and the source of the funds used (whether separate or community).

As referenced above, another common marital interest present in many states was previously discussed in Chapter 3 — the *tenancy by the entirety*. A tenancy by the entirety is similar to a joint tenancy with right of survivorship, but can generally only be created between a husband and a wife. In effect, this form of property ownership adds a fifth unity — marriage — to the four traditionally required for a joint tenancy with right of survivorship (time, title, interest, and possession). Unlike the joint tenancy with right of survivorship, however, a tenancy by the entirety cannot be severed unilaterally by one of the spouse co-owners. Instead, a tenancy by the entirety will ordinarily only come to an end upon the death of one of the spouses, a divorce, or by agreement of the two spouses. Accordingly, unlike for other jointly owned property, a partition action would be unavailable. The tenancy by the entirety is recognized by slightly fewer than half the states, and is typically not present in community property states.

Finally, there are far fewer property law protections for unmarried couples whether they are of the opposite sex or the same sex. As to the latter, although a few states have recognized same-sex marriages or property law protections through civil union statutes, most states have not done so.

EXERCISE 5-1 — SEPARATE v. COMMUNITY PROPERTY

GENERAL DESCRIPTION OF EXERCISE: Addressing legal questions involving marital property issues in separate and community property states; considering issues involving migrating couples.

SKILLS INVOLVED: Fact analysis and development, statutory research and analysis, creative problem solving, preparation for a client meeting and a phone call to a client, preparation of a client letter.

PARTICIPANTS NEEDED: Tasks 1, 4, and 5 are individual projects, and Tasks 2, 3, and 6 are collaborative and require two or more students each.

ESTIMATED TIME REQUIRED:

Task 1: 30 minutes to analyze

Task 2: 30 minutes to analyze and 30 minutes to prepare a letter

Task 3: 1.5 hours — 30 minutes to view video and analyze; 30 minutes to prepare an informal memorandum; and 30 minutes to brainstorm solutions with classmate(s)

Task 4: 1.5 hours to analyze and prepare brief memoranda (approximately 30 minutes for each of the three subparts)

Task 5: One hour to analyze

Task 6: 45 minutes to analyze and draft bill language

LEVEL OF DIFFICULTY (1-5):

ROLES IN EXERCISE: You are acting as a law clerk in a law firm or as a lawyer for the parties as identified in the first five tasks. In Task 6 you are working for a state senator.

THE EXERCISE: 5-1

Assume that Howell and Wilma, who have been married for forty years, have been lifelong residents of Illinois. In 1975, Howell bought a farm west of Peoria in the vicinity of Farmington. The deed to the farm named Howell Smithers as the grantee. Wilma was not named in the deed, but she and Howell worked the farm until a year ago. Having had their fill of Illinois winters and the difficult challenges of farming, they decided to retire and move away. Howell sold the farm for $600,000 and invested the proceeds partially in stocks and bonds, and the rest in a certificate of deposit at Bank of America. Ownership was registered in his name, and he did not make any payable on death elections with respect to the accounts. Consider the following:

TASK 1:   Sadly, Howell died a week after completing the foregoing transactions. He and Wilma had not completed their plans as to where they were going to move. After selling the farm, they had been staying in Peoria with Howell's son Ned and his family. Ned is 48 years old, and was born during Howell's first marriage to Wendy. Howell and Wilma also had a son during their long marriage, but he died in a car accident when he was a teenager. Assume that Wilma has come to see you with a problem. She has brought you a copy of Howell's will, which he had executed just over four years ago. In his will, Howell included the following relevant provision: "I leave my farm to my dear wife Wilma. I leave all the rest, residue, and remainder of my property to my son Ned." Wilma is uncertain about her rights given that the farm has now been sold. You have told her that you would do some research and call her within a few days. Your task is to review the referenced e-materials for Task 1 on the **LexisNexis Webcourse**, and prepare some talking points for your follow-up phone conversation with Wilma. You may assume that the couple had few additional assets between them. Wilma owns approximately $20,000 worth of personal property, and Howell owned another $10,000 in personal property.

TASK 2:   Assume, instead, that Howell did not die as described in Task 1 above. Instead, he and Wilma moved from Illinois to Bellevue, Washington, where they rented a condo. They enjoyed their time in the Pacific Northwest, but Howell died approximately a year after their move. As in Task 1, assume that Howell never got around to changing his will. Wilma has shown you the will, and she is uncertain about her rights given that the farm was sold more than a year ago. As with the prior task, you have told Wilma that you would do some research and get in touch with her within a few days. Your task is to review the referenced e-materials for Task 2 on the **LexisNexis Webcourse**, and prepare a letter to Wilma that summarizes your assessment. Draft the letter and meet with a classmate to exchange letters and compare your results.

TASK 3:   Assume, instead, that Howell has not died, and that he and Wilma are staying with his son in Peoria, Illinois, for a few weeks after the closing on the sale of the farm. Rather than the Seattle area, they are contemplating a move to San Antonio, Texas. In fact, they have made one trip to the area and found a lovely, brand-new garden home, which they are very interested in purchasing. The new home, which has every conceivable amenity, will likely cost $500,000. They are also thinking about buying a new luxury car for making the trip south, which will cost an additional $50,000. In addition, for purposes of this task and unlike the facts in the first two tasks, you are to assume that Howell's will provides, in pertinent part:

I devise (1) one-fourth of my entire estate to my loving wife Wilma, (2) one-half of my entire estate to my son Ned, and (3) the remainder of my estate to the American Red Cross.

You have learned that Wilma's sister Nadine lives in Dallas. She has apparently told Wilma that Texas is a community property state and that Wilma should know her rights before she and Howell move to San Antonio. Assume that you are the junior associate in a small law firm in Illinois. Wilma has called the managing partner in your law office and wants to come by the office for a discussion about any legal issues about which she should be made aware. Your boss is in trial this week and has asked you to meet with Wilma. Your task is to view the client interview video and the cited materials located in the e-materials for this chapter on the **LexisNexis Webcourse**. Then, prepare an informal memorandum to your boss that summarizes your assessment of the legal issues. Once you have drafted your memorandum, meet with one or two classmates to discuss your respective findings. Then, your group should brainstorm about possible recommendations that your firm can make to Wilma to protect her rights and interests.

TASK 4:   Rather than the facts above, assume that Hank lives and works in the Palo Alto, California, area. In 2002, he purchased a $300,000 term life insurance policy from the All-Risk Insurance Company. He agreed to pay $100 per month for the premiums on the policy. Accordingly, his premiums were $1,200/year. Because Hank was single and had no children, he designated his mother, Martha, as the beneficiary of the policy. Assume that Hank has continued to pay the premiums on the policy out of his earnings, and that the cost of the premiums for the policy has remained constant. In 2006, Hank fell in love with Winifred, and they were married. However, Hank never thought to contact All-Risk to change his beneficiary designation. Sadly, it is now 2012, and Hank was recently killed in a freak motorcycle accident on his way to work. Winifred was surprised to find out that Hank had a life insurance policy, and she was even more surprised to learn that Martha was named as the beneficiary. She has asked you about her rights, if any, with regard to the policy proceeds.

(a)   After reviewing the referenced e-materials for this task on the **LexisNexis Webcourse**, prepare a brief memorandum that addresses Winifred's query. (For purposes of your analysis, you may assume that out of the ten years that Hank made payments on his insurance policy, he was single for the first four full years, and married to Winifred for the remaining six years.)

(b)   Would your analysis change if all of the foregoing events transpired near Round Rock, Texas, as opposed to the Palo Alto area? Prior to making your assessment, review the e-materials for this subpart on the **LexisNexis Webcourse**.

(c)   With respect to the foregoing, what if all the events took place near Round Rock, Texas, but (1) the order of the events was switched, and (2) the insurance policy was not a privately secured policy, but instead was an employee benefit paid for each month by a payroll deduction from Hank's monthly earnings? That is, Hank and Winifred married in 2002. Hank then took a job with his employer in 2006 and elected to have $100/month of his salary go toward the premiums on a $300,000 term life insurance policy via a payroll deduction. As in subparts (a) and (b), he identified his mother, Martha, as the beneficiary of what he considered to be his insurance policy. Assess the extent of Winifred's rights, if any. There are also links in the e-materials for this subpart on the **LexisNexis Webcourse**.

TASK 5:   Rather than the facts in Task 4 above, assume that Hank, then a resident of Reno, Nevada, took out a $300,000 term life insurance policy directly from All-Risk Insurance Co. in 2006. (Accordingly, unlike in Task 4(c), this insurance policy was not part of an employee benefits plan.) Hank paid the first two annual premiums in 2006 and 2007 of $1,200 each out of his savings account. Hank was divorced at that time, but had a daughter, Daphne, from his first marriage. Hank designated Daphne as the beneficiary of this insurance policy. In 2008, Hank married Winifred. He paid the $1,200 annual premiums in both 2008 and 2009 out of the couple's joint checking account from earnings from both of their jobs. In early 2010, Hank and Winifred moved from Reno to take high-tech jobs in the Round Rock, Texas, area. Thereafter, Hank continued to make the $1,200 annual premiums in 2010 and 2011 out of joint earnings. Hank then died in early 2012 (before the 2012 premium was due). The insurance beneficiary was never changed. As in Task 4, Winifred has asked you to assess her rights, if any, with regard to the insurance proceeds. After reviewing the referenced e-materials for this task on the **LexisNexis Webcourse**, prepare a brief memorandum that addresses Winifred's query.

TASK 6:   Assume that you are working for a Texas state senator. She has reminded you that Texas, which is a community property state, has created the concept of *quasi-community property* for divorce in the case of migrating couples who have moved to Texas from a separate property state. She is concerned that some married couples (and companies) might be reluctant to relocate to Texas because the state does not apply the quasi-community property concept at death. She would like you to consider statutes from several other states (linked in the e-materials for this chapter on the **LexisNexis Webcourse**) and to draft some bill language that would extend the reach of the quasi-community property concept to the death of a spouse. Work with a classmate to develop and draft some appropriate bill language.

EXERCISE 5-2 — TENANCY BY THE ENTIRETY

GENERAL DESCRIPTION OF EXERCISE: Addressing legal questions involving a tenancy by the entirety or joint tenancy with right of survivorship.

SKILLS INVOLVED: Case and statutory analysis, creation of a memorandum for a supervising attorney.

PARTICIPANTS NEEDED: Two students

ESTIMATED TIME REQUIRED:

Task 1: One hour — 30 minutes to prepare and 30 minutes to prepare a memorandum

LEVEL OF DIFFICULTY (1-5):

ROLES IN EXERCISE: You are acting as a law clerk in a law firm.

THE EXERCISE: 5-2

Assume that Hansel and Willeen are residents of Virginia and have been married for eight years. They have run into some financial problems and face the prospect of filing for bankruptcy. They have numerous individual, separate debts (totaling just over $100,000 between them) and one significant joint debt — their home loan. In fact, their principal asset is their home, which has an appraised value of $350,000. They still owe $240,000 on their mortgage, and the debt is secured by a mortgage lien against the property. Assume that you are working for a law firm that Hansel and Willeen have retained. Their matter has been assigned to Susan, a second-year lawyer who went to law school in the northeast. Susan has told you that based on her meeting with Hansel and Willeen, she understands that the couple owns their home as tenants by the entirety. In fact, the recitals on the deed to the property and information in the loan documents all reflect that the property is held by the couple as a tenancy by the entirety. Earlier today, Susan told you the following,

> I really don't remember much from first-year property about tenancies by the entirety. In fact, because they weren't recognized in our state, my professor didn't say much about them. I'd like to know how they might be treated in a bankruptcy proceeding. Also, I need to know whether it matters when the property was actually purchased. The couple showed me the deed that recites that the property was purchased as tenants by the entirety, but the date of the deed is a few weeks prior to the date they got married. When I asked them about it, Willeen remembered that they "might have done the paperwork" on the house purchase "a week or two before the wedding so that we could move right in after our honeymoon. It was great because Hansel was able to carry me over the threshold of our new home when we got back from Branson!"

Susan would like you to review the cases, statute, and secondary materials that are linked on the **LexisNexis Webcourse** for this Task and prepare her a brief, informal memorandum that addresses her two questions. Please do so. After you have prepared your assessment, exchange it with a classmate and compare and discuss your respective results.

Chapter 6

NON-VOLITIONAL PROPERTY INTERESTS

INTRODUCTION

Non-volitional (natural) interests arise merely because a person owns real property. They are not based on the affirmative actions or inactions of a person such as a conveyance, because of implication, or by prescription. The common law developed doctrines to describe the extent of a person's rights and duties as well as to adjust competing claims of other property owners, non-property owners, and society in general. These rules may vary considerably among jurisdictions and can be the subject of extensive codification.

Nuisance.

A nuisance arises when a property owner uses his or her property in a manner that unreasonably interferes with the ability of another property owner to use and enjoy his or her property. A use of property which is merely annoying or disturbing is not enough to be a nuisance. Instead, the use must be unreasonable to a person of ordinary sensibilities.

It is important to distinguish nuisance from trespass. A trespass action is a method a property owner uses to protect the right of the owner to have exclusive occupation of the property he or she owns. To succeed in a trespass action, it is not necessary to show that the land was damaged. Instead, it is sufficient that an unauthorized physical intrusion has occurred. On the other hand, a nuisance action protects a property owner's ability to use and enjoy property. Actual harm is required but a physical intrusion, while it might exist, is not required. The complaining person does not need to show that the property owner was at fault; no finding of intentional, knowing, reckless, or negligent conduct is required to win a nuisance action.

Courts examine a variety of factors to determine whether a property owner has committed a nuisance by using the property in an unreasonable manner. These factors may include (1) the suitability of the property owner's use of the property to the location of that property, (2) whether the use is authorized by applicable zoning laws, (3) whether the use existed before the person asserting the nuisance purchased his or her property, (4) the social utility of the alleged nuisance, and (5) the cost of avoiding the harm either by the offending property owner stopping the offending activity or the complaining property owner selling the property and moving away from the nuisance.

If the court finds a nuisance exists, the court may issue an injunction to prevent the property owner from continuing with the offending conduct. With respect to past harm, the court may award compensatory damages to the complaining property owner. In some cases, the court will permit the nuisance to continue but will require the offending property owner to provide monetary compensation for the future harm.

Support of Land.

A property owner has the right to have his or her land supported by the land surrounding it, both on the sides (lateral support) and beneath (subjacent support).

It is easy to envision *lateral support* issues if you think about parcels of land located on a hill. The lower property owner has a duty to support the upper property owner's land. If the lower property owner removes support and the upper land slips, even if the removal of support is not done in a negligent manner, most courts will deem the lower property owner responsible for the damages that ensue. Generally, the courts do not extend liability to buildings or other improvements because the duty of the lower landowner is to support the land only in its natural condition. Likewise, the lower landowner has no obligation to take affirmative steps to protect the upper land so that if the land slides on its own due to rain, wind, earthquake, etc., the lower landowner is not responsible. If the lower landowner removes natural support and replaces it with artificial support such as a retaining wall, then the lower landowner is typically responsible to maintain the artificial support.

Subjacent support issues arise when ownership of the surface of the property is separated from ownership of the underground or mineral rights. The owner of the underground interest has a duty to provide support for the surface of the property. Courts take different positions on whether the duty is to support the land only in its natural state or with the buildings that have already been built on the property. With respect to some types of mining, especially coal, there are extensive state and federal regulations regarding how much underground support is required (that is, how much coal must be left in place as pillars to support the surface).

Water.

A property owner has rights and obligations with respect to three types of water: surface water, water in watercourses, and groundwater.

Surface water is water that does not flow in a well-defined channel such as run-off from rain or melting snow. A property owner may have rights and duties with respect to retaining surface water as well as disposing of it. With regard to retention of surface water, most courts follow the rule of capture, which means that the first landowner who retains the water flowing across his or her land may keep it and become its owner regardless of on whose property the rain or snow originally fell. Once the water flows over the property owner's land and onto another person's land, the ability of that landowner to become the owner of the water is lost.

Three main approaches have developed regarding the disposition of surface water. With the *natural flow* rule (also called the *natural servitude* or *civil law* rule), each landowner has the right to have water flow naturally away from the landowner's property as well as the duty to allow water coming from other land to flow over the property owner's land. In other words, landowners are responsible if they alter the natural contour of their land so that water leaves the land or cannot enter the land in a way different from how the water flows in nature. Because this approach makes land development difficult, some courts that follow the natural flow rule have created an exception for reasonable changes to the natural contour.

The second approach is the *common enemy* rule, which treats surface water as a threat to every property owner's land. Thus, a landowner may take whatever steps are necessary to remove surface water or prevent surface water from entering the property, even if doing so causes harm to other property owners' lands. Because artificial discharges could decimate the land of lower property owners, many courts following the common enemy rule have created an exception for unreasonable conduct.

The third approach is the *reasonable use* rule, which examines the property owner's conduct to see if the steps taken (e.g., trenches dug or barriers erected) are reasonable under the circumstances. In many respects, this approach treats the conduct of a property owner as a possible nuisance and examines the conduct in a similar manner.

Water in watercourses is water which runs in a well-defined channel such as a stream, river, or lake. Note that the Commerce Clause of the United States Constitution gives the federal government control over navigable waterways and these rights are superior to private rights. In our discussion, we are looking at basic concepts and are not factoring in the federal government's extensive regulation of navigable water.

Two basic systems are used in the United States to govern rights to water. The first of these is the *riparian* system, which is used primarily by states located east of the Mississippi River as well as some states to the west. Rights to water under the riparian system arise because a person owns land that is (1) physically adjacent to the watercourse and (2) located in the same watershed as the watercourse. A person who does not own riparian land generally has no rights to the water.

A riparian landowner's rights to the water depends on the landowner's use of the water and the impact that use has on lower (downstream) riparians. A riparian has an *absolute right* to take (1) any quantity of water for any purpose if taking the water does not effect the quantity, quality, or velocity of the flow once the water reaches the land of the adjacent lower riparian, and (2) water for domestic purposes such as drinking and bathing even if doing so reduces the flow. Disputes may arise over whether a certain use is domestic. For example, irrigating a small garden may be permitted but not irrigating a field of growing crops.

A riparian may also have *correlative rights* to use the water for nondomestic purposes. Courts have developed two main approaches to determine allowable nondomestic use. The first approach is the *natural flow rule* which, although developed at common law, is now a minority approach. Under this approach, the upper riparian may use water for nondomestic use only if the natural flow of the water is not altered. The second and majority approach is the *reasonable use rule* which permits an upper riparian to impact the water flow as long as doing so is reasonable when compared to the rights of the lower riparian.

The second basic watercourse system in the United States is *prior appropriation*, which is used primarily in arid states west of the Mississippi River. Under this system, owning property adjacent to a watercourse may not automatically give the property owner rights to the water. And, conversely, a property owner whose land is not adjacent to the watercourse may obtain rights to the water. Traditionally, a person obtains a right to water by demonstrating that the person has used that quantity of water in the past. Under modern law, the government issues permits for the use of a certain amount of water. In times of water shortage, the date of prior use or the application or recording of a government permit controls who has priority to use the water.

In some prior appropriation states, all rights to water are controlled by the prior appropriation system. In other words, riparian rights are abolished. States using this method are often referred to as adopting the *Colorado doctrine*. However, in some prior appropriation states, there is an uneasy coexistence of riparian rights and prior appropriation rights. States adopting this method are said to follow the *California doctrine*.

Groundwater is water that filters down from the surface and is now contained in an aquifer or other underground formation. States have developed three approaches for determining the ownership of groundwater. The common law followed the *rule of capture*, which means that the owner of the overlying land owns the water and can withdraw any quantity of water for any purpose even if it causes the water to drain from beneath surrounding property resulting in the wells on the nearby properties running dry. However, a landowner may neither take the groundwater maliciously with intent to injure the owner of surrounding land, nor use the water in a wasteful manner.

The second approach is the *reasonable use rule*, also called the American rule. Under this approach, the courts look at the reasonableness of the property owner's use of the groundwater and evaluate it by balancing the competing interests of the landowners.

The third approach is *prior appropriation*, which operates in a similar manner to the prior appropriation system for water in watercourses.

Oil and Gas.

Under the law of most nations, the national government owns the oil and gas beneath its citizens' property. However, in the United States, a property owner may have rights to the oil and gas beneath his or her property. Generally, oil and gas is not owned until it is actually produced, as its movement through underground formations is deemed secret, occult, or concealed. However, some states treat the property owner as owning the oil and gas even though the property owner may later lose that oil and gas though a producing well on surrounding property. States that adopt this approach often do this so they can enhance the value of the property for appraisal purposes and thus levy a higher property tax.

Airspace and Sunlight.

The common law courts often said that a person owned the space above his or her land to the periphery of the universe. However, this principle evolved before modern technology gave rise to skyscrapers, aircraft, solar power, cloud seeding, communication signals, artificial satellites, and the like. Thus, modern law has had to adjust the rights of the property owner to account for these modern developments. Unfortunately, the law has been far from uniform in these areas.

EXERCISE 6-1

GENERAL DESCRIPTION OF EXERCISE: Carefully examine fact patterns regarding the rights to various non-volitional property interests, conduct research, draft advisory memos or letters.

SKILLS INVOLVED: Fact analysis and development, creative analysis regarding untouched areas of law based on existing law, identifying consequences of various parties' actions, drafting letters or memos.

PARTICIPANTS NEEDED: Only one participant is needed for the following tasks.

ESTIMATED TIME REQUIRED:

Task 1: 2 hours to examine pictures, conduct research, and draft a memo.

Task 2: 2 hours to consider the rule of capture as it applies to the facts given and draft a judicial opinion.

Task 3: 2 hours to review the facts and applicable law and then draft a memo.

Task 4: 1 hour to review facts and prepare a client letter.

LEVEL OF DIFFICULTY (1-5):

ROLE IN EXERCISE: In Tasks 1, 3, and 4, you are an attorney specializing in natural property interests. In Task 2, you are a judge who needs to decide a dispute involving groundwater.

THE EXERCISE

TASK 1:   Your longtime client and close friend, John Snow, owns a small ranch in a rural area. For 25 years, he has used an old, refurbished windmill to pump water from his underground well into an above ground storage tank. He uses this windmill because it saves him money on electricity and he loves the rustic look it adds to his ranch home.

About five years ago, John's neighbor of 15 years passed away, leaving his property to his grandson. The grandson, a greedy entrepreneur and thief in John's opinion, moved in with his family and has slowly been building a large number of various sized water-pumping windmills on the property. John thinks the new windmills are tacky, unsightly eyesores that ruin the beautiful landscape. He is also positive that the large number of the bigger windmills, which are upwind from his property, are the reason his smaller single windmill is not pumping water as efficiently as it has in the past. However, John is still able to pump all the water he currently needs.

John also believes that the upwind "windmill farm" his neighbor has built consisting of massive electric-generating turbines is also stealing John's share of the wind. Before his new neighbor arrived, John had the only windmill within a 10-mile radius; now there are dozens littering his neighbor's property.

Review the pictures on the **LexisNexis Webcourse** supplementing this Task depicting John's and his neighbor's windmills. Based on the pictures, John's circum-stances, and your knowledge of water and wind law, determine whether your client, as the original windmill owner, has a first priority right to the wind and/or water.

Prepare a letter to John detailing your findings and opinions. To conduct your research, consider applying the law of the specific state in which you intend to practice. Otherwise, prepare your memo from the perspective of a state that does not have prior law on these issues.

TASK 2:   You are a district court judge in a small, rural county. The state in which your county resides is a rule of capture state for groundwater. A motion for summary judgment, with the following facts and issues, is currently before your court.

Four local landowners, collectively members of the Sparrow Family, have brought a civil action against Great Lakes Bottling Company, a/k/a Spring Natural Drinking Water Co., for negligent drainage of the landowners' water wells. Because this is a motion for summary judgment, you may assume the following facts are true.

In 2011, Spring began pumping 75,000 gallons of groundwater a day, seven days a week, from land near the Sparrows'. The groundwater is then processed at the Great Lakes Bottling Company plant, located on the same property, and used in commercial production of bottled water. A few weeks after pumping started, the Sparrow's wells were almost totally depleted. The Sparrows are seeking injunctive relief against Spring, as well as actual damages and punitive damages for alleged nuisance, negligence, gross negligence, and malice by Spring.

Spring asserts that the law does not recognize any of the Sparrows' claims because the land is located in a rule of capture state. On the other hand, the Sparrows claim their suit falls within recognized rule of capture exceptions. The Sparrows also ask you to throw out the rule of capture and replace it with the rule of reasonable use.

Based on your knowledge of property law and the facts of this case, how should you decide? After reading the two cases provided on the **LexisNexis Webcourse** for this Task, draft the opinion you would issue.

TASK 3: Mary, a lifelong California resident, has the right to receive sunlight across the real property directly in front of her home by way of a valid solar easement. This easement was granted to her in 2005, under the Solar Easement Law, California Civil Code § 801.5. A link for information about this law is provided on the **LexisNexis Webcourse** for this Task. Through this easement, Mary is protected from any structure on the property directly in front of her home that might block her ability to receive sunlight for her solar panels. The solar panels, installed in 2005, are the primary source of energy for Mary's home.

Big Corporation owns real property close to Mary's home. It has begun construction of a fifty-story high rise — a pricey job that will cost Big Corporation $750 million to finish. Unfortunately, Big Corporation's attorneys did not diligently research the property before construction began. One-third of the new high rise falls within Mary's solar easement.

An attorney for Mary has sent Big Corporation a letter notifying them of the existing easement and threatening to sue for injunctive relief if Big Corporation does not change its construction plans.

As the brightest attorney for Big Corporation, the CEO has come to you for advice. The CEO believes the easiest thing for Big Corporation to do is continue construction. He firmly believes Mary's attorney is bluffing and will not file suit to keep the construction project from going through.

Draft a memo to the CEO of Big Corporation outlining your opinion as to whether Big Corporation should continue with its construction plans and the likelihood that Mary's suit to stop construction would prevail under her solar easement. In addition, develop other options for Big Corporation short of altering construction plans and the enormous cost that would entail.

TASK 4: You are an attorney representing a client in a potential waste suit. You are responsible for counseling your client on the client's potential liability.

Three adjacent pieces of land, owned by three separate and constantly feuding neighbors, sit on top of one common pool of oil. Over 60% of the common pool lies beneath the land of one owner, Sarah.

The owners are in a race to be the first one to tap the large underground oil pool that flows beneath their lands. Sarah is the first landowner to complete her well successfully, and begins drilling immediately. Peter is in a close second but has run into some serious funding issues that threaten to cease his entire operation. Joanie is a life tenant in the property, the elderly guardian of her 6-year old grandson, to whom the property was bequeathed by the grandson's late parents but who will not gain the rights to manage the property until Joanie passes away. Joanie has begun construction of two wells on the property.

As Sarah begins to recover oil from the common pool, Joanie finishes construction of both wells and begins to draw more oil from the common pool than Sarah. Frustrated with the slow construction process, Peter decides to cut corners in an effort to speed up construction. His time-saving measures work and the well begins to draw oil from the common pool. However, the corners Peter cut caused the well to blow out, resulting in the collapse of a large portion of the common pool. Now all three owners are unable to draw oil at a commercially reasonable cost from underneath their properties.

Sarah has come to your firm as a frustrated landowner. She would like to sue both of her neighbors for trespass and theft of her oil. She would also like to sue Peter for negligent destruction of her property. Assume that Sarah, Peter, and Joanie (in her capacity as a life tenant), all own the surface and mineral rights to their respective parcels of property.

Write a letter to Sarah outlining the likelihood she has of recovering from either Joanie or Peter. As you write the letter, think of how this entire problem could have been avoided from the beginning.

If the state in which you intend to practice produces oil commercially, use the law of that state for your letter. If your state does not produce oil in commercial quantities, apply the law of one of the major oil producing states such as Texas.

Chapter 7

ESTATES & FUTURE INTERESTS

INTRODUCTION

The common law system of land ownership has a long and rich history. Understanding the feudal system from which modern forms of land ownership arose is, despite being fascinating, beyond the scope of this brief review. Instead, this review is designed to provide a basic summary of the types and characteristics of different estates and future interests, recognizing that these traditional forms of ownership and the rules applicable to them are often changed by modern statutes and judicial developments.

Interests or estates in property are divided into two main categories, freehold and non-freehold. *Freehold estates* arising out of the free tenures of common law are the focus of this chapter. *Non-freehold estates* such as tenancies are discussed in Chapter 8.

Interests in property are classified based on whether the owner of the property interest has a current right to possess the property. If the owner may currently occupy the property, the person is said to own a *present interest*. If the person must wait until some later time to possess the property, the person is said to own a *future interest*.

At common law and persisting in various degrees today, the precise wording used in the grant of the property determines the type of interest being transferred. The language in a grant is divided into two categories. The first is *words of purchase* which indicate the person who is receiving the grant of property. The second is *words of limitation* which identifies the type of interest being transferred. Unfortunately, the words of limitation do not expressly state the type of interest. Instead, you must "translate" the words of limitation into the type of interest being transferred. As you examine a grant of land, you must ascertain the type of words used and then identify the type of interest being granted. Once you have accomplished this task, you can then determine the characteristics of the grant and the rights and obligations of the owner.

As you read this introduction, refer to the two charts below which may be helpful in visualizing the relationships between and among the various interests.

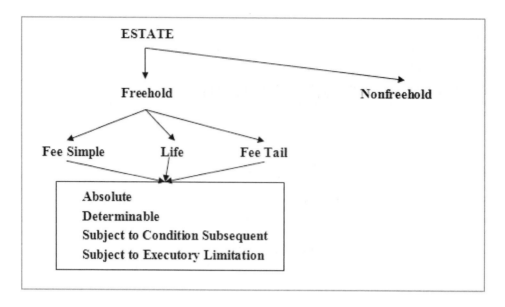

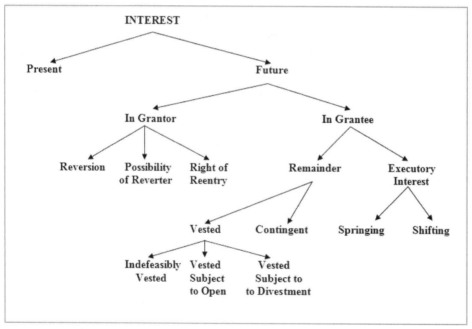

The largest estate known at common law is the *fee simple absolute*. This estate consists of the greatest number of "sticks" from the "bundle of sticks" forming rights in property that society allows a person to own. The owner of a fee simple absolute estate has the right to possess and use the property from now until death and the right to transfer that property while alive by gift or sale. Property owned in fee simple absolute passes at the owner's death by intestate succession to the owner's heirs or by will to the person or persons the owner designates.

At common law, special language was needed to transfer a fee simple grant. The grant needed "and [his] [her] heirs" as words of limitation to transfer a fee simple. However, most states today do not require these words of limitation and instead treat a lack of words of limitation as creating a fee simple. At common law, the default interest when a grant lacked words of limitation was a life estate.

A *life estate* is an interest which the owner has only while the owner is alive. Immediately upon the owner's death, the property passes to another person. The standard words of limitation to create a life estate are "for life." A life estate owner may transfer the life estate to another person but that person will have rights only for the life of the original life estate owner. A life estate which is measured by the life of another person is called a *life estate pur autre vie*. When the owner of the life estate, the life tenant, dies, the property will pass to the holder of the future interest in the property such as the original owner via a reversion or to another person via a remainder.

Because the owner's interest is only for life, the owner owes duties to the holder of the future interest. These include the duty as to keep the property in repair, not commit waste, pay property taxes, pay interest (but not principal) on a mortgage, and allow reasonable inspection by the owner of the future interest.

A *fee tail* is a grant which keeps property in the ownership of the lineal descendants of the owner indefinitely. In effect, a fee tail is an unending series of life estates and is created by using words of limitation such as "and the heirs of [his] [her] body" or "and [his] [her] issue." The original owner retains a future interest, a *reversion*, because it is possible that all lineal descendants "die out" so that there is no one left to own the property. Fee tails are disfavored under modern law and are deemed invalid as against public policy in many states because they are viewed as "tying up" property for an impermissibly long period of time.

A grant of land may also be conditioned in some manner making the owner's interest defeasible. In other words, the owner's interest is not absolute but instead could be lost if a stated condition is satisfied. There are three main types of defeasible estates. The first is the *fee simple determinable* which contains words of purchase such as "so long as [condition exists]," "until [condition occurs]," or "while [condition exists]." If the owner violates the condition, the grantor regains the property through a future interest called a *possibility of reverter*. At common law but not always under modern law, the divestment of the owner of a fee simple determinable occurred immediately upon the condition occurring even if the owner of the possibility of reverter did not take steps to evict the former owner.

The second type of defeasible estate is the *fee simple subject to a condition subsequent*. The words of limitation creating this type of estate are in the "if. . . then" format, such as "but if [condition occurs], then" "provided that if [condition occurs], then," or "on the condition that if [condition occurs], then." The grantor's retained interest is called either a *right to reenter* or a *power of termination*. At common law and typically under modern law, the divestment of the owner of a fee simple subject to a condition subsequent does not occur automatically upon the breach of the condition, but instead requires the grantor's affirmative action. Thus, the grantor may forfeit the right to regain ownership by waiver or estoppel.

The third type of defeasible estate is the *fee simple subject to an executory limitation*, which provides that upon breach of a condition, the property does not go back to the grantor but instead passes to another person. The common law did not recognize executory interests until 1535, and thus, this is a relatively "modern" type of property interest. No special words of limitation are needed as long as the grant provides for the property to pass to a third party upon breach of the condition.

Now let's turn our attention to future interests, that is, a property interest which does not give the owner the present right to use or occupy the property. Instead, the owner hopes that the time will come when the person will obtain the right to occupy the property. There is no guarantee that such a time will ever occur.

When classifying a future interest, the first step is to determine whether the owner is the original owner (the grantor) or is a third party (a grantee). There are three types of future interests which a grantor may retain: (1) a reversion following a life estate, fee tail, or lease, (2) a possibility of reverter following a fee simple determinable, or (3) a right of reentry/power of termination following a fee simple subject to a condition subsequent.

If the future interest is in the hands of a third party, it is either a *remainder* or an *executory interest*. To determine which type of interest, you should first determine if it meets the requirements of a remainder. If it does, it is a remainder and then you can further classify it into one of three subtypes. If the interest does not qualify as a remainder, then it is an executory interest and you can then classify it into one of the two subtypes.

The key characteristics of a remainder are that the interest (1) must become possessory immediately upon the expiration of the prior estate (no gaps), and (2) cannot shorten or divest a prior estate (the prior estate must end "naturally," such as by the death of the life tenant, and thus cannot follow a condition subsequent).

Once you determine the interest is a remainder, you must further classify the remainder as vested or contingent. A *vested remainder* is a remainder where it is ascertainable with certainty that the owner of the remainder will be entitled to possession when the proceeding estate terminates. There are no conditions precedent to the owner of the remainder obtaining possession other than the prior estate naturally ending. Thus, you can "touch" the owner of the interest because the owner is born and identifiable and the interest is not subject to a condition precedent. On the other hand, with a *contingent remainder* there is only a conditional possibility of ever obtaining possession of the property. You cannot currently "touch" the owner of the interest because the owner, for example, is unborn or unascertainable or the interest is subject to a condition precedent which has not yet occurred.

If you determine the remainder is vested, then you should determine the type of vested remainder. An *indefeasibly vested remainder* is one in which the owner will obtain possession of the property when the prior estate ends and there is nothing that can stop that from occurring. A *vested remainder subject to open (partial divestment)* is one in which the owner will obtain possession of the property when the prior estate ends but may receive a smaller share than anticipated because the owner will need to share with additional individuals. For example, the grantor may have transferred the remainder to a class such as a particular person's children and the person is still alive and thus could have additional children. A *vested remainder subject to total divestment* is one in which the owner might not obtain possession because of a condition subsequent ("but if") which either does or does not occur.

If a future interest in the hands of a third party does not meet the requirements of a remainder, typically because there is a gap between the expiration of the prior estate or the interest will prematurely divest a prior estate, the interest is an *executory interest*. If the interest will divest a prior interest held by a grantee, the interest is a *shifting executory interest*. On the other hand, if it divests the grantor of a retained interest, the interest is a *springing executory interest*.

Under the law of most states, the Rule Against Perpetuities prohibits interests in which the ability to ascertain the identity of a person in whom an interest in the property will vest is delayed beyond a specified period of time. This Rule is based on several policy grounds such as to prevent the undue restraint on the transfer of property, to keep the property marketable, and to limit dead-hand control of property. Only future interests that are contingent and not held by the grantor are subject to the Rule. Thus, the only interests that require a Rule Against Perpetuities analysis are (1) contingent remainders, (2) vested remainders subject to open, and (3) executory interests.

At common law, and still in many states today, this time is twenty-one years after the death of some life in being at the time of the creation of the interest, plus a period of gestation.

The application of the Rule Against Perpetuities is restricted in many cases. Most, if not all, jurisdictions limit the application of the Rule to private property interests; certainty in vesting is not required for interests which are charitable. Some states reject the common law approach of voiding the grantee's interest if there is any possibility, no matter how unlikely it may be, that a contingency could occur that would delay vesting beyond the perpetuities period. Instead, they have adopted a *wait-and-see* approach and look at how vesting actually occurs instead of how it could occur under "wild-eyed hypotheticals." Other jurisdictions lengthen the period or permit the courts to reform the interest using *cy pres*; that is, the court may modify the interest to make it fit within the Rule while still carrying out the grantor's intent as closely as possible. Many states have enacted the *Uniform Statutory Rule Against Perpetuities Act* which combines many of these reforms, such as a ninety-year time period from the time of the grant (rather than the death of the lives in being) plus wait-and-see and deferred-reformation components.

About one-half of the states have completely abolished or substantially reformed the Rule with regard to trusts (but not necessarily with regard to other types of property interests). In these states, settlors may create *dynasty trusts* which last indefinitely and restrict benefits to remote descendants of the settlor. The decision to abolish the Rule in these states was, at least in part, an economic decision to encourage wealthy settlors to bring their property into these states, establish trusts, employ local trustees and attorneys, and pay local taxes.

The list of links on the **LexisNexis Webcourse** for this chapter contains a link to an extensive series of questions and answers designed to test your knowledge of the classification of estates and future interests.

EXERCISE 7-1

GENERAL DESCRIPTION OF EXERCISE: Review deeds, wills, and the specific facts of the case to determine what interest(s) the deeds created and their validity.

SKILLS INVOLVED: Critical reading of deeds and wills and evaluating their provisions to determine the types of interests they grant; writing legal memos.

PARTICIPANTS NEEDED: Only one participant is needed for the following tasks.

ESTIMATED TIME REQUIRED:

Task 1: 2 hours to review a deed, conduct research, and prepare a memo.

Task 2: 2 hours to review a deed, conduct research, and prepare a memo.

Task 3: 2 hours to review a will, conduct research, and prepare a memo.

LEVEL OF DIFFICULTY (1-5):

ROLE IN EXERCISE: You are a law clerk at a prestigious local firm. The senior partner has asked you to review deeds containing problematic language. You are to review the deeds and applicable law, and prepare a memo highlighting the issues raised by each deed.

THE EXERCISE

APPLICABLE LAW:

Although each of the properties in the three tasks below are set in a particular state, assume that the property is located in the state in which you intend to practice.

TASK 1: Access the deed for Task 1 as provided on the **LexisNexis Webcourse** for this Task. You may assume that the deed is properly executed and recorded.

As you review this deed, pay close attention to the following facts: Matt Hawkins has recently died and Jack Bryan's three children are arguing over the meaning of a particular provision in the deed. John Bryan, the eldest, has a J.D. from The Ohio State University but received a Bachelor's of Arts in Public Relations from the University of Michigan. Joe Bryan is currently enrolled at The Ohio State University as a junior engineering major who plans to graduate in May of next year. Jane Bryan, the youngest of Jack's children, is a high school senior in Ohio. She has been accepted to The Ohio State University and plans to attend in the fall but has not yet enrolled.

Determine what estates and future interests the deed purports to grant and explain fully in a memo to the senior partner. Identify all possibilities and explain differing interpretations and options.

TASK 2: Access the deed for Task 2 as provided on the **LexisNexis Webcourse** for this Task. You may assume that the deed is properly executed and recorded.

As you review this deed, pay close attention to the following facts: At the time Zachary conveyed the property to Brent Michaels, Mr. Michaels was a premed and biology major at University of Nevada at Las Vegas. Since then, Brent Michaels received his Ph.D. in Philosophy from Pepperdine University in December 2010. He is currently a Professor of Philosophy at UNLV and specifically demands that both his students and colleagues call him only by the name, "Dr. Michaels."

At the moment, Zachary, Brent, and Axel all claim that they are entitled to current possession of the property. Prepare a memo explaining the basis of each person's claim and how you believe a court would resolve the dispute.

TASK 3: William Bell's will contains the following language:

> I hereby direct my Executor, Olivia Dunham, to sell all of my real property for cash and to invest the proceeds in safe and secure tax-free U.S. government bonds or insured tax-free municipal bonds. This trust is to be called the James Madison Fund to honor our fourth President, the Father of the Constitution. The ultimate purpose of this fund is to provide a million dollar trust fund for every American 18 years or older. At 6% compound interest and a starting figure of $1,000,000.00, it would take approximately 346 years to provide enough money to do this. My executor will head the Board of Trustees. When the Fund reaches $15,000,000, my Executor's function will cease, and the money will be turned over to the Sec. of the Treasury for management by the federal government. The President of the U.S., the Vice-President of the U.S., and the Speaker of the U.S. House of Representatives shall be permanent Trustees of the Fund. The Congress of the United

States shall make the final rules and regulations as to how the money will be distributed. No one shall be denied their share because of race, religion, marital status, sexual preference, or the amount of their wealth or lack thereof.

I leave the remainder of my estate to Walter Bishop.

Walter claims that the devise of real property is void, while the state Attorney General claims that the devise is valid as a charitable gift. Both parties agree that the will is valid; the dispute is only over the validity of the devise.

You are clerking for the judge who has to render a decision. Prepare a memo to the judge explaining the arguments that Walter and the Attorney General will make. Then, provide your opinion as to which party has the better theory.

Chapter 8

LANDLORD/TENANT

INTRODUCTION

This chapter will address problems pertaining to landlord-tenant law. Most of the major Property casebooks cover a broad array of topics involving landlords and tenants, including historical leasehold estates, discriminatory actions by landlords, delivery of possession, transfers to subsequent tenants, abandonment and eviction, and condition of the premises. This chapter will include exercises that focus on certain selected issues from this wide array of topics. There are many other issues pertaining to landlord-tenant law, but these areas cover most of the important, major topic areas.

Leasehold estates

We addressed estates and future interests in real property in Chapter 7. These are sometimes referred to as freehold estates. Over time, four types of non-freehold — or leasehold — estates developed at common law. These leasehold estates — or *tenancies* — include (1) the *term of years tenancy*, (2) the *periodic tenancy*, (3) the *tenancy at will*, and (4) the *tenancy at sufferance*.

The *term of years tenancy*, as the name suggests, is a leasehold estate that will last for some fixed period that is established by agreement in advance, such as six months, one year, five years, 99 years, or some other fixed period. There was no limit on the stated period at common law. Today, many commercial leases and residential leases will fall under this category. Once the lease term ends, the leasehold interest will expire as of the last date of the stated term. The tenant's right to possession will expire as of that date, and no notice of termination is necessary.

In contrast to the term of years tenancy, a *periodic tenancy* is a form of leasehold interest that continues for a period of fixed time that is automatically renewed for successive periods until notice is provided by *either* the landlord or tenant to terminate the arrangement. Common examples include a "month-to-month" tenancy or a "year-to-year" tenancy. Under common law rules, a month's notice was necessary to terminate a month-to-month tenancy. In addition, the notice had to be provided by the end of the preceding period, and not at some point in the middle. Thus, if a month-to-month tenancy began on the first day of a month, the month's notice of termination was necessary by the last day of the preceding month. If, however, either the landlord or tenant gave notice of termination on, for example, the tenth day of the month, then the tenancy would continue for the rest of that month, as well as all of the next month. In contrast, many states now have statutes that allow termination of a month-to-month tenancy at any time upon 30 days notice. For longer periods, such as the "year-to-year" tenancy, common law rules required notice of at least half of the period, or six months in the case of the year-to-year tenancy. This period has also been shortened in some states by statute.

The *tenancy at will* provided for no fixed period and would last so long as both the landlord and tenant desired. At common law, if the lease allowed for termination at the will of one of the parties, it was construed to be correspondingly terminable at the will of the other party. That rule has been modified by modern courts which have attempted to carry out the drafter's likely intent. At common law, no notice of termination was necessary, but modern statutes typically require some form of advance notice prior to termination — often 30 days or the interval between rent payments. The death of a party or abandonment by the tenant can also result in termination.

The final type of leasehold estate, the *tenancy at sufferance*, typically involves a so-called holdover tenant. That is, at the end of the stated lease term, the tenant remains in possession — even though there is no longer a valid right for that party to be in possession. It is a form of wrongful occupancy. The landlord traditionally has had two options — either evict the holdover tenant or consent to an agreement (either expressly or impliedly) for a new tenancy. If a tenant nonetheless tenders the next month's rent, and the landlord cashes the check, then the landlord presumably will be deemed not to have elected to evict, and to have consented to a new tenancy. But, there is uncertainty as to whether such actions result in a renewal or extension of the original term, or an implied creation of a month-to-month periodic tenancy. The results tend to vary by jurisdiction. Many states have adopted statutes that address this situation. Some limit any renewed tenancy to a year, absent express agreement, and others authorize the landlord to collect double rent from a holdover tenant.

Discriminatory actions in the rental of property

Most of the major casebooks address statutory prohibitions against discriminatory actions in the leasing of property. The two key federal statutes are (1) the Civil Rights Act of 1866, 42 U.S.C. § 1982, and the Fair Housing Act of 1968, as amended, 42 U.S.C. §§ 3601, et seq. (Links to these acts are included in the **LexisNexis Webcourse** for this chapter.) The older of these statutes, 42 U.S.C. § 1982, forbids racial discrimination in the leasing (or sale) of property. In turn, the Fair Housing Act, as amended, addresses discrimination in the leasing (or sale) of property based on race, color, religion, sex, familial status, national origin, or disability. The Fair Housing Act provisions are, accordingly, broader than the 1866 Civil Rights Act because the older statute addresses only racial discrimination. In some ways, however, the Fair Housing Act provisions are narrower in scope because they include exceptions to the Act's discrimination provisions for single family homes rented by the owner or rentals within "quadplexes" or smaller in which the owner lives in one of the quarters. By way of contrast, however, these exceptions do not apply to additional provisions in the Fair Housing Act that prohibit discriminatory advertising about the rental or sale of property.

Delivery of possession

Issues also arise with respect to a landlord's obligations regarding *delivery of possession* to a tenant. Suppose that T is a college student who has signed a one-year lease with L to rent a house that is set to begin on September 1. But, when T shows up with her belongings on September 1, the former tenant, Z, has not moved out. Assume further that the lease was silent concerning L's duty to deliver possession to T. Jurisdictions are split on resolution of this issue. Under the so-called English rule, the landlord not only must deliver legal possession at the start of the lease term, but has an implied obligation to deliver physical possession at the same time. In our hypothetical situation, in an English-rule jurisdiction, T would be able to terminate the lease and sue L for damages, or could maintain the lease, pay no rent until L took steps to remove Z, and seek damages from L. Other jurisdictions, however, apply the so-called American rule, and do not imply an obligation on the part of the landlord to deliver actual physical possession at the start of the lease term. These jurisdictions are of the view that tenants should insist on a delivery-of-possession clause in the lease. Accordingly, if our hypothetical scenario arose in a jurisdiction that applies the American rule, T would have no recourse against L, and would instead have to sue Z, the holdover tenant, to obtain possession and seek damages. Although jurisdictions remain divided, the English rule likely represents the majority view regarding this issue.

Transfers to subsequent tenants

There are situations in which a tenant will wish to depart from the leased premises prior to the end of a lease term and transfer interests in the property to a substitute tenant. Typically, the tenant will want to do so and be relieved of future responsibility for paying rent under the lease, but that will likely run counter to the landlord's interests. Consistent with the general principle that property interests are usually considered to be freely alienable, tenants are generally able to transfer their lease rights to a substitute tenant by either an *assignment* of the lease or via a *sublease* arrangement. Under the majority view, a transfer by a tenant to a third party of all the tenant's remaining rights and interests under the lease is considered to be an *assignment*. Often, this is determined formalistically by assessing whether the tenant has transferred all of the remaining lease term to the substitute party. In contrast, if the tenant transfers anything less than the full remaining term, the transfer is considered to be a *sublease*. For example, if T has two years remaining on a three-year lease with L, and then transfers T's leasehold interests to T1 for a term of nine months, this would be considered to be a sublease. Correspondingly, if T transfers the full remaining two-year interest to T1, the arrangement would be viewed as an assignment. In contrast to the foregoing, in a minority of jurisdictions, the courts instead focus on the likely intent of the parties in trying to ordain whether the parties intended either an assignment or a sublease.

Characterization of the transfer as either an assignment or a sublease can have implications with regard to liability issues. In the foregoing example, when L and T entered into their three-year lease, they had a *privity of contract* relationship via their agreement and under contract law. Under property law principles, they also had a *privity of estate* relationship. Stemming from feudal days, we would say that T had a right to possess and occupy the land, which carried with it certain rights and duties connected with having an interest or estate in the land. When T transfers all the remaining term to T1 via an assignment, T is no longer in privity of estate with L (because T1 now has the full remaining right and interest in the leasehold estate as a total substitute for T). But, absent a *release* by L or *novation* of the original lease agreement, T remains in privity of contract with L. That is, should T1 default on the lease provisions, L could still pursue a remedy for breach against T. Moreover, L would have a cause of action against T1 because of L and T1's privity of estate relationship. In the case of a sublease, however, L remains in privity of estate with T because T will not have transferred *all* of the remaining term and interests in the leasehold estate to T1. (L will remain in privity of contract with T, as well, given the lease agreement between L and T.) Correspondingly, T and T1 will themselves have a privity of estate relationship because T is in effect acting as a landlord vis-à-vis T1 through T's sublease to T1. If L seeks damages from T for T1's default or breach of the sublease, then T will likely be liable and will need to pursue an action against T1. Moreover, there are further complications relating to these issues for either an assignment or a sublease if T1 makes an affirmative promise to *assume* the provisions of the original lease. In such a situation, then T1 is also in a privity of contract relationship with L because T1 has either made a direct promise to L to meet the obligations of the lease, or L is an intended third party beneficiary of such a promise made by T1 to T. A privity of contract relationship will allow L to seek remedies directly from T1 even in the case of a sublease in which there is no privity of estate between L and T1.

Many leases include provisions that disallow a tenant to assign or sublease the tenant's rights under the lease without obtaining written consent of the landlord. Some states have statutes to this effect, as well. Historically, the courts upheld a landlord's refusal to grant consent to an assignment or sublease for any reason unless the lease provision included a standard for denying consent. Recent cases, however, in situations primarily involving commercial leases have engrafted a limitation on landlords from denying such consent absent a commercially reasonable basis.

Abandonment and eviction

An *abandonment* occurs when a tenant unjustifiably vacates the premises prior to expiration of the lease term and defaults on the payment of rent. Under traditional rules, the landlord could (1) treat the abandonment as a surrender of the lease, and thereby terminate the lease, (2) leave the leased property vacant for the rest of the lease term and then sue for accrued rent, or (3) mitigate damages by re-letting the leased premises, and then seeking any lease amounts not otherwise obtained from the substitute tenant. Correspondingly, there was no obligation to mitigate damages. By way of contrast, today, the vast majority of jurisdictions impose a duty on a landlord to mitigate damages, and the landlord is left with the two choices of lease termination or the mitigation of damages.

With regard to a landlord's *eviction* of a tenant for breach of a lease, the common law allowed the landlord to retake possession by using self-help provided that the landlord used no more force than was reasonably necessary. The use of self-help, however, is strongly disfavored under modern law. Instead, most jurisdictions require that a landlord evict a tenant only by means of judicial process. Most states have enacted statutes that provide expedited procedures for processing eviction suits in the courts.

Condition of the premises

The major Property casebooks address two principal issues pertaining to the condition of leased premises: *constructive eviction* and the *implied warranty of habitability*. At common law, because the tenant obtained an interest in land, the tenant also was viewed to have the duty to make repairs to the leased property. Over time, however, courts began to recognize a form of protection for the tenant in the case of substantial problems with the leased premises. The courts created an *implied covenant of quiet enjoyment*, which precludes the landlord from wrongfully interfering with the tenant's possession and enjoyment of the property. Over time, this implied covenant was extended to situations involving substantial impairments to a tenant's enjoyment and use of the property (such as a significantly leaky roof, flooding of the leased premises, etc.). The tenant could then assert that the breach of the covenant of quiet enjoyment was so significant that it was tantamount to an actual eviction, and thus should be deemed to be a *constructive eviction*. This would allow the tenant to vacate the premises justifiably without a continuing responsibility for payment of rent.

As a separate doctrine, modern courts have created the concept of the *implied warranty of habitability*. Under this doctrine, a landlord has a duty to maintain leased premises in a habitable condition. The implied warranty relates to significant defects with leased premises and is imposed to assure that the premises meet minimum conditions for being fit for human habitation. Because the courts (and a few legislatures) have created this warranty, most have also held that the implied warranty cannot be waived by a clause in the lease.

EXERCISE 8-1

GENERAL DESCRIPTION OF EXERCISE: Addressing legal questions involving a tenant who abandons the leased property and a tenant who appears to be in violation of a "no pets" provision in a written lease.

SKILLS INVOLVED: Fact analysis and development, developing facts for the drafting of a complaint, case research and analysis, preparation for a telephone call or meeting with opposing counsel, drafting a letter to opposing counsel.

PARTICIPANTS NEEDED: These tasks are collaborative and require two students each.

ESTIMATED TIME REQUIRED:

Task 1: 1 hour and 30 minutes to assess facts, review forms, and develop a list of needed information

Task 2(a): 30 minutes to analyze and 30 minutes to discuss with classmate

Task 2(b): 1 hour to draft letter

LEVEL OF DIFFICULTY (1-5):

ROLES IN EXERCISE: You are acting as a lawyer for a party as identified in the various tasks.

THE EXERCISE: 8-1

For Tasks 1 and 2(a) below, assume that your firm's client owns an apartment complex in Minnetoba City, which is located in the state of Minnetoba. The complex includes 40 apartments, which are comprised of one-bedroom and two-bedroom units. The complex is named Lakeside Apartments, and is owned by Lakeside Properties, Inc. — your client. Lakeside's agent, Lori Leece, serves as the manager for the complex, and she lives on-site in one of the units.

TASK 1: Assume that Lori contacted you in mid-July on behalf of Lakeside with regard to a problem with a tenant. The tenant, Tim Tennant, had a written lease for apartment unit 17A through August 31. Tim was a college student at the nearby Minnetoba State University. Unfortunately, he had earned very poor grades during the spring semester and decided that he was going to leave town and move in with his girlfriend "up-state." Tim did not pay his rent at the first of June. When Lori dropped by his apartment on June 3 to ask about his rent, she was surprised to see him packing up his belongings. When Lori mentioned that he had not yet paid his rent, Tim burst into tears, and told her that because of his poor grades he was moving out. Lori reminded him about his lease obligations, but he told her that he just could not bear to stay any longer near the scene of his academic failure. He quickly proceeded to move all of his things out of the apartment and into his car, and then slipped his apartment keys through the slot on Lori's door.

The monthly rent under Tim's lease was $1,000 per month. Lori has relayed that per her employer's established policies for attempting to mitigate damages, she promptly began advertising the unit's availability. However, because the area in which Lakeside Apartments is located caters primarily to college students, demand is relatively low during the summer months. The apartment sat empty for the month of June. Finally, over the July 4 weekend, Lori was able to enter into a new lease with Terrie Tuttle, who was in town looking for housing. Because Terrie was about to start law school, and orientation is set to begin at Minnetoba State Law in mid-August, Terrie desired a lease that would begin on August 15. Because Lori had no other units available until September 1, Terrie was very interested in unit 17A. Lori offered to rent unit 17A at the rate of $1,000 per month to begin on August 1, but Terrie said that she did not need the apartment until August 15. After some negotiation, Terrie agreed to begin a 13-month lease on August 1, but to pay only $700 for the first month, and $1,000 per month thereafter. That was acceptable to Lori.

Lori has now contacted you about pursuing a remedy against Tim for his breach of the lease agreement. In addition to his failure to honor his rental obligations for the summer months, Lori also discovered that Tim had apparently caused damage to the apartment. There were several cigarette burns in the carpet and grease stains on the walls near the stove. In addition, it appeared that Tim had not engaged in any cleaning activities during the lease term. Lori has told you that the repair and cleaning costs have totaled $2,000, but Tim's security deposit was only $1,000.

Your task is to review the materials that are linked in the **LexisNexis Webcourse** for this task and, working with a classmate, develop a list of the additional facts that you will need to gather to be in position to draft a complaint for damages against Tim Tennant.

TASK 2(a):   Assume that several weeks have passed. Lori Leece has just called you regarding an issue with another tenant. Teddy Seales lives in unit 21B under the terms of a two-year lease. The lease, like all other leases for Lakeside Apartments, has a "no pets" provision. Lori has seen Teddy with a yellow Labrador retriever dog over the last week or two. When Lori confronted Teddy about the presence of the dog, Teddy replied that he was a veteran who had served in Afghanistan, and that he needed Trixie, his dog. When Lori reminded Teddy that the lease does not allow pets, Teddy asserted that Trixie was *not* a pet, and that officials at the Veterans Administration (VA) had recommended that he acquire a service animal. Teddy did not elaborate further.

Your task is to review the materials that are linked in the **LexisNexis Webcourse** for this task and, working with a classmate, determine (1) whether there are any legal exceptions to the "no pets" policy, and, if so, (2) what additional facts should be elicited to be able to advise Lori appropriately.

TASK 2(b):   For purposes of this exercise, assume that you are a volunteer lawyer working with a local Veterans' Legal Assistance program. Lori Leece has told Teddy that he is in violation of his lease and must no longer keep Trixie at the apartment unit. Teddy has sought your legal assistance. He has told you that the doctors at the VA have diagnosed him with Post-Traumatic Stress Disorder (PTSD), and strongly recommended that he obtain a service animal. He also informed you that Trixie is a specially trained animal, and received her training from a recognized, reputable dog training organization.

Your task is to review the materials that are linked in the **LexisNexis Webcourse** for both this Task and Task 2(a) above and to draft a letter on Teddy's behalf to Lori Leece at the Lakeside Apartments explaining why Lakeside is required by law to make an exception to its "no pets" policy as a reasonable accommodation for Teddy's disability. Then, exchange letters with a classmate. Compare your approaches and discuss any differences.

EXERCISE 8-2

GENERAL DESCRIPTION OF EXERCISE: Addressing legal questions involving landlords and tenants.

SKILLS INVOLVED: Fact, case, and statutory analysis, creative problem solving, preparation for negotiation, negotiating on behalf of a client, preparation of a client letter

PARTICIPANTS NEEDED: These tasks are collaborative. Tasks 1, 2, and 4 require two students for each, and Task 3 requires four students.

ESTIMATED TIME REQUIRED:

Task 1: One hour — 30 minutes to analyze and 30 minutes to discuss with classmate

Task 2: One hour — 30 minutes to prepare and 30 minutes to draft

Task 3: 30 minutes to analyze and 30-45 minutes to negotiate

Task 4: One hour — 30 minutes to analyze and 30 minutes to discuss with classmate

LEVEL OF DIFFICULTY (1-5):

ROLES IN EXERCISE: You are acting as a lawyer for the parties as identified in the various tasks.

THE EXERCISE: 8-2

The following factual scenarios pose several types of recurring issues involving landlord-tenant disputes. Although you can address Tasks 1, 2, and 4 on an individual basis, we recommend that you work with a classmate as described for each problem.

TASK 1: Lonnie is the owner of a two-story building in downtown Urbano, a college town in upstate Minnetoba. The building is located in a quaint business district not far from the local college. A restaurant, named Good Bistro, occupies the first floor of the building. Additionally, there are three small residential apartments upstairs. Tina, who is a first-year law student at the nearby college, has leased one of the three apartments for a year at $700/month rent. Tina moved in at the end of August, and all went well for the first two months. In early November, however, Lonnie hired a new manager, Mel, for Good Bistro. Mel promptly changed the closing time for Good Bistro from 9:00 p.m. to 2:00 a.m., and he converted one of the back dining rooms to a combination martini bar and cigar lounge. He also changed the name of the establishment to Good Bistro & Sports Bar. (Urbano has a local ordinance that bans smoking in restaurants, but includes an exception for sports bars.)

Tina is furious and wants out of her lease. Her exams are fast-approaching, and she is very unhappy about the late night noise and cigar smoke. She has found a comparably sized apartment about six blocks away, but the rent is $100/month higher. Assume that you are a recent law school graduate who just passed the state bar exam. You are Tina's friend, having met her earlier in the fall while dining at Good Bistro. When Tina told you about her current issues with Lonnie and her living situation, you agreed to represent her on a pro bono basis. You also have learned that Lonnie has a local lawyer who handles disputes with tenants. Your task is to review the materials that are linked in the **LexisNexis Webcourse** for Task 1, and then to prepare a list of talking points for a meeting with Lonnie's attorney regarding Tina's desire to get out of her lease and perhaps seek damages. Then, exchange your list with a classmate and discuss your respective approaches.

TASK 2: For purposes of this task, assume that several months after the foregoing scenario, Lonnie decided to lease the entire downstairs space in his building to Mel. The Good Bistro & Sports Bar had been very successful under Mel's management, and Lonnie decided that he no longer needed to be an on-site owner/operator. Accordingly, Lonnie and Mel agreed to a three-year lease of the commercial property for Mel to continue operating Good Bistro & Sports Bar. Lonnie would no longer have any interest in the business, and would solely be Mel's landlord. The lease called for an annual rent of $36,000, payable in $3,000 monthly installments. All went well, and the business continued to thrive. After two years, Lonnie and Mel attempted to negotiate an extension, but the efforts failed. The lease included no language discussing the possibility of renewals or extensions. There were no further discussions about an extension.

Assume that the three-year lease period then ended on March 31. Nonetheless, Lonnie received a $3,000 check from Mel on April 1, which he promptly endorsed and deposited. The same thing happened on May 1. On May 10, however, Lonnie learned about interest in the space from a national restaurant chain, Big Chain Dining. The chain offered to enter into a three-year lease with a higher rent than the arrangement with Mel. Lonnie's attorney has now contacted Mel and told him to clear out because his three-year lease has expired. Mel has come to you to ask for your help. Your task is to review the materials that are linked in the **LexisNexis Webcourse** for Task 2, and to draft a letter to Lonnie's attorney, Alice Advocate, explaining Mel's rights. Then, exchange your letter with that of a classmate and discuss any differences in your respective approaches.

TASK 3:   Suppose that after receiving the letter that you wrote for Task 2, Alice Advocate shared it with her client, Lonnie. Three days later, Alice called you and indicated that she and Lonnie would like to meet with you and Mel to discuss a possible resolution of the issues that have arisen.

Located in the **LexisNexis Webcourse** for this part of the exercise are (1) confidential instructions for counsel for Lonnie and (2) confidential instructions for counsel for Mel. Your professor will assign you to work in pairs and for each pair to represent either Lonnie or Mel. After reviewing and considering the legal issues and the guidance from your client(s), you are to (1) develop your plan and strategy for a negotiation session with counsel for the opposing side; (2) engage in a negotiation with the pair of students who are representing the opposing side — your professor will identify the match-ups for the negotiation sessions; and (3) draft a memorandum of agreement if you are able to reach a settlement during the negotiation session.

TASK 4:   Suppose that the parties in Task 3 reached a settlement agreement in which Lonnie and Mel agreed to a four-year lease extension at an increased rental rate. About a year later, the same national restaurant chain, Big Chain Dining, again appeared on the scene. They still very much like the location of Good Bistro & Sports Bar and would like to convert the space to one of their restaurants. In fact, Big Chain Dining has made an attractive offer to Mel to buy out his business and to obtain an assignment from him of the remaining three years of the lease with Lonnie. When Mel reviewed his lease, he spotted the following clause, "Tenant agrees not to sublease, transfer, or assign this Lease to any third party without prior written consent of Landlord." Mel then contacted Lonnie who expressed quite a bit of reluctance to grant permission. Lonnie told him, "I'm not much of a fan of chain restaurants." Mel has contacted you and asked for your help.

Your task is to review the materials set forth in the **LexisNexis Webcourse** for Task 4 and to develop arguments and a strategy for persuading Lonnie and his counsel to provide consent for the lease assignment. Prepare a short memorandum outlining your arguments. Then, exchange your work and ideas with a classmate and discuss any differences in approach.

Chapter 9

LAND SALES — TRANSACTIONS

INTRODUCTION

One of the most significant legal transactions that individuals will encounter in their lifetimes is the purchase or sale of a home or other real property. In addition, commercial property transactions are also very common. We will address the acquisition or sale of land over the next three chapters. Chapter 10 will cover topics relating to marketable title, real estate closings, and deeds; Chapter 11 will focus on problems pertaining to title assurance in real estate transactions, as well as adverse possession issues; and this chapter will concentrate on basic issues in land sale transactions.

Statute of Frauds.

As you learned (or will learn) in your Contracts course, most oral agreements are enforceable; however, statutes require certain types of contracts to be in writing. Every state has enacted so-called statutes of frauds that require written agreements for certain types of transactions to be enforceable. One of the more important of these statutes relates to real estate agreements. In general, the sale of an interest in land must be in writing to be enforceable. Accordingly, an oral agreement for the sale of an interest in land is generally unenforceable. Typically, to be enforceable, there must be a *writing* — whether formal or informal — which contains the *key terms* of the agreement (such as an adequate property description, the identity of the parties, and the price), and the writing must be *signed* by the party against whom enforcement is sought. Agreements that violate the statute of frauds are not void, but they are *voidable*. That is, a party who is disputing the enforceability of an agreement must raise the statute of frauds as a defense.

The statutes of frauds were traditionally intended to guard against fraud and to discourage perjury. Over time, however, the courts have developed exceptions and rules of interpretation to ameliorate the perceived harshness of rigidly applying the statutes in certain situations. For example, the courts have recognized an exception for *partial performance* of an otherwise unenforceable oral agreement, and an exception based on *estoppel* when a party has substantially relied to his or her detriment on an agreement that would otherwise be unenforceable because of the statute of frauds. Many courts also allow various writings to be tacked together to comprise the writing necessary to satisfy the statute, and still other courts view the signature requirement as not being particularly demanding and recognize substitutes such as pre-printed letterhead, marks, or symbols.

Form Contracts.

At one time, attorneys typically handled most real estate transactions. Today, that is still often the case with regard to commercial real estate transactions, but in many parts of the country, it is very unusual for residential real estate sales. Instead, real estate brokers or agents provide prospective buyers with pre-printed, standard form contracts that include blanks for terms such as price, financing method, dates for performance, and conditions. Typically, a prospective buyer will then fill out the form with desired terms, and present the "contract" — which is really just a written offer — to the seller for consideration. The seller can accept the offer by signing the proffered contract, or can reply with a counter-offer. Often, the counter-offer is made on the same document by lining out the prospective buyer's terms and inserting the seller's desired terms. This process will continue until the parties reach agreement (or not). A lawyer will generally not be involved until after the agreement is reached and often solely in regard to title work or deed preparation. In many states, however, members of the bar or a State Bar committee will have drafted the standard forms. Additionally, if a dispute arises, the parties will then often turn to a lawyer for professional assistance.

Conditions.

There is a strong likelihood that a real estate contract will include one or more conditions. For example, a prospective buyer will often insist on a condition that makes the buyer's commitment contingent on obtaining financing. Most courts hold that if the buyer makes a good faith and diligent effort to find financing, yet is unsuccessful, the buyer can avoid the contract and recover any deposit. The prospective buyer might also include a condition that the contract is contingent on the buyer's sale of an existing residence. The purchaser will also likely insist on a condition that makes the sale contingent on the completion of one or more satisfactory inspections. Language about inspections is ordinarily included in the standard, pre-printed form contract. Another form of condition is a *time is of the essence* clause. If the contract of sale makes time of the essence, a late performance by one party will excuse the other party from any further obligation to perform. If the contract contains no such provision and thereby does not make time of the essence, a late performance by one party — if not unreasonable — will not excuse the other party from performance. The party who is late will be liable for damages, if any, for the tardiness, but the breach is not a "total" breach. Because delays are not unusual in real estate transactions, often a time is of the essence clause is not included.

One other type of condition that is present in real estate contracts involves the nature of the title that the seller is conveying. The parties should and typically will include language in the contract requiring that the title must be of a certain quality. In this regard, such contracts will often call for the seller to provide either a marketable or an insurable title. In the absence of such a provision, however, the courts generally imply a condition that, at the closing of the transaction, the seller must provide evidence that the title is marketable. A "marketable" title is one that is free from reasonable doubt and free from reasonable risk of legal attack. Because the subject relates more to the closing of the real estate transaction, it will be addressed in greater detail in Chapter 10.

Duty to Disclose.

Under the traditional view, the doctrine of *caveat emptor* (let the "buyer beware") controlled, and a seller of real property had no duty to make disclosures to a prospective buyer about defects in the property. Over time, exceptions arose for a seller's affirmative misrepresentations, active concealment of defects, or a situation in which the seller owed a fiduciary duty to the buyer. Today, however, courts in most jurisdictions require the seller to disclose material defects that impact the value of the property which are known to the seller but are not known and not readily discoverable by the buyer. Also, there are some state and federal statutory requirements that direct sellers to make certain disclosures about their property. By way of contrast, most courts do not impose a duty on a buyer of real property to disclose facts about the property known to the buyer, but not to the seller, absent some form of fiduciary duty between the parties.

Equitable Conversion.

What happens if there is a loss to the real property (e.g., by fire or hail) after the contract for sale is executed, but before the closing? Courts traditionally applied the doctrine of *equitable conversion* in this type of situation. Under that doctrine, the buyer is treated as the equitable owner of the property as soon as the contract is signed, and — as the owner — is viewed as bearing the risk of any loss to the property from the date of contract execution. Given, however, that a seller generally remains in possession of the property until the time of closing, this doctrine often appeared to run counter to the parties' likely expectations. Accordingly, today, it is quite common for the real estate contract to place the risk of loss on the seller until the time of closing and to require the seller to maintain insurance through that time.

The equitable conversion doctrine is also relevant if either the seller or buyer dies after contract execution and prior to the closing. Just because a party to the contract has died, the contract itself is still valid. It remains a contract right that can be enforced by the administrator of the estate of the deceased on behalf of the heirs or devisees of the deceased. (Or, if the estate is administered rapidly, the heirs or devisees may enforce the agreement themselves.) If the seller dies prior to the closing, the doctrine of equitable conversion treats the deceased seller's interest in receiving the proceeds of the sale as *personal property* for purposes of inheritance laws. Correspondingly, because an equitable interest in the real property was transferred to the buyer at the time of contracting, if the buyer dies before closing, the buyer's interest is considered to be an interest in *real property* for purposes of the inheritance laws, even though the closing has not yet occurred. Accordingly, if the seller dies, the seller's estate has a duty to convey the property to the buyer, and the proceeds of the sale must go to the estate administrator and be treated as personal property. In contrast, if the buyer dies prior to closing, the buyer's interest will descend as real property to the buyer's heirs or devisees. Issues and tensions can arise if the deceased buyer, for example, has a will that leaves all of his or her personal property to X, but all real property to Y. Y would inherit the land that was subject to the contract. And, if the jurisdiction applies the doctrine of *exoneration of liens*, the administrator of the buyer's estate will first have to pay the purchase price out of the personal property assets of the estate — assets that would otherwise have gone to X! A number of states have eliminated or altered the exoneration of liens doctrine by statute, but it remains in place in some states.

Financing.

For obvious reasons, most real estate purchasers cannot pay cash for the full amount of a home or other real property, and must accordingly finance their purchase. Most of you will have only a brief introduction to real estate financing in your Property course, but an advanced course in Real Estate Finance and Transactions is offered at most law schools. We will provide a brief overview here.

Typically, an institutional lender will loan money for the purchase price to the prospective buyer. The buyer will then sign a written *note* promising the lender to repay the loan. To obtain a *security interest* to secure the borrower's repayment, the lender will require the borrower to provide a *mortgage* to the lender. (It should be noted that a few states follow an approach to mortgage law called the *title theory*, which has its roots in the English common law view of mortgages. Under that theory, the lender/mortgagee is considered to hold legal title to the property until such time as the mortgage debt is fully satisfied. Most states, however, follow the *lien theory* of mortgages. That is, the purchaser/borrower has legal and equitable title to the real property, and the borrower/mortgagee has a security interest or lien only.)

If a borrower defaults on the loan, the lender has the right to foreclose on the loan through a statutorily prescribed foreclosure process. Many states require a judicially supervised sale. Other states allow the borrower to grant the lender/mortgagee a power of sale, which bypasses the need for judicial proceedings. Typically, foreclosure is by a public sale, and proceeds of the sale are used to pay off or be applied toward the mortgage debt. If the sale proceeds are greater than the debt owed, the surplus goes to the debtor/borrower. If, however, the sale provides less than the amount owed, in many jurisdictions, the lender can seek a judgment for the deficiency against the borrower. Some states, however, have enacted *anti-deficiency* statutes that preclude or restrict the lender's ability to obtain a deficiency judgment against the borrower.

By way of contrast, in many states the buyer/borrower instead provides a *deed of trust* to a third-party (the *trustee*, who is often the lender's officer or attorney) as security for the lender (the *beneficiary*). If the borrower defaults on the loan, the trustee will pursue statutorily prescribed foreclosure procedures and provide the proceeds from the public foreclosure sale to the lender. As a practical matter, today there are not significant differences between the deed of trust and a mortgage with the power of sale.

Another somewhat common method of real estate financing is the *installment land contract*, which is also sometimes known as a *contract for deed*. Under an installment land contract, the buyer makes a promise to pay the purchase price to the property seller in installments over a stated period of time. There is no third-party lender, and the seller is, in effect, acting in the role of a lender. In fact, it is sometimes called *seller financing*. Although the buyer takes possession of the property after closing, the seller retains the title to the property until the installment payments are fully made. Only after all the payments are complete will the seller transfer a deed to the buyer. These contracts have traditionally allowed the seller to regain possession of the property in the event of default by the buyer, with the seller retaining all payments previously made. This remedy is known as a *forfeiture*. At one time, such installment land contract forfeiture provisions were routinely enforced. Today, however, given the potential harshness of such a remedy, most courts (and some legislatures) have limited the enforcement of forfeiture clauses in a variety of ways. In fact, many states treat the buyer's equitable rights in an installment land contract in a comparable fashion to a mortgage or deed of trust.

Remedies for Breach.

If either the seller or buyer breaches a real estate contract, the non-breaching party can generally seek either specific performance or damages. Accordingly, in the event that a seller declines to go through with an agreement to sell land, the aggrieved buyer may consider pursuing specific performance. Because each parcel of land is considered to be unique and money damages are often not an adequate remedy, courts are generally quite willing to grant specific performance. In addition to specific performance, the unhappy buyer can also seek consequential damages for delays caused by the seller's breach. Alternatively, the buyer could seek money damages under an expectation theory. The usual rule for buyer's damages after a breach by the seller is the difference, as of the date of the breach, between the market price and the contract price. If the seller has re-sold the property to a third party at a higher price, the courts can take the resale price into account as strong evidence of the market price at time of breach. This approach allows the buyer's remedy to include any profit the seller accrued through the re-sale. To be made whole, the aggrieved buyer can also seek restitution of any deposit money.

If, on the other hand, the buyer breaches the agreement and refuses to conclude the transaction, the seller is entitled to seek either specific performance or sue for damages. If the seller pursues an order for specific performance, the court's decree should address both payment by the buyer, and a transfer of the title from the seller to the buyer. If the seller, alternatively, seeks money damages, the usual formula for calculating damages is — as with a buyer's breach — the difference between the contract price and the fair market value at the time of the breach. The seller also has a duty to mitigate damages. Nonetheless, if the seller re-sells at a lower price than the contract price, the courts will often treat the re-sale price as strong evidence of the market price if the re-sale was made in good faith. Alternatively, in the event of the buyer's breach, the unhappy seller may retain any *earnest money* (deposit or down payment) paid by the buyer at the time of contract formation as liquidated damages. The general rule is that, even in the absence of an express liquidated damages provision in the contract, the seller may retain the earnest money as a form of liquidated damages given the difficulties of establishing damages with certainty and a wide acceptance of deposits that typically do not exceed 10 percent of the purchase price. A minority of courts, however, will allow the breaching buyer to seek restitution of any amount by which the deposit exceeds the seller's actual damages, unless the contract expressly establishes the earnest money deposit as constituting liquidated damages in the event of the buyer's breach. (You no doubt have or will consider the validity and enforceability of liquidated damages clauses in your Contracts course.)

EXERCISE 9-1

GENERAL DESCRIPTION OF EXERCISE: Addressing legal questions involving contracts for the sale of real property.

SKILLS INVOLVED: Fact analysis and development, analysis of standard form contract terms, case research and analysis, preparation for counseling a client, drafting a contract clause and drafting a contract amendment.

PARTICIPANTS NEEDED: These tasks are collaborative and require two students each.

ESTIMATED TIME REQUIRED:

Task 1: 45 minutes to review forms and assess additional information needed from the client

Task 2: 45 minutes to analyze and draft clause and 15 minutes to discuss with classmate

Task 3: One hour — 30 minutes to analyze and 30 minutes to discuss with classmate

Task 4: One hour to analyze and draft amendment and 15 minutes to discuss with classmate

Task 5: One hour — 30 minutes to analyze and 30 minutes to discuss with classmate

LEVEL OF DIFFICULTY (1-5):

ROLES IN EXERCISE: You are acting as a lawyer for a party as identified in the various tasks.

THE EXERCISE: 9-1

The following factual scenarios involve issues pertaining to real estate contracts for residential property. Assume that you are a recent graduate of Minnetoba State Law School, and that you have been practicing at a small law firm in Minnetoba City for about a year.

TASK 1:   One of your old friends from college, Paul Purchaser, has learned that you are practicing law, and he has contacted you asking for your help on a matter. Paul is single, in his mid-twenties, and is employed as a high school math teacher. He owns a small condominium, but has decided to buy a house. Over the weekend, he fell in love with a house located at 5412 Laurel Lane in Minnetoba City. The sellers, Val and Vernon Vendor, do not have a realtor, and the house is listed as "for sale by owner." Paul also does not have a realtor. He saw an advertisement for a Sunday afternoon open house for the home in the classified section of the Minnetoba Bugle Sunday newspaper. Paul is unsure about how to make a "legal" offer on the home. He called Val and Vernon on Sunday night and told them that he wanted to buy the house, and he indicated a price range that he would likely be willing to pay. However, he is uncertain about how to proceed. To avoid commission charges, he does not want to hire a realtor. He found what appears to be a form real estate contract while surfing on the web, but he was uncertain about what to do next. Accordingly, Paul has asked you to review the form contract and assist him in making an offer to buy the house — whether by using that contract or something else.

Val and Vernon have advertised a price of $240,000 for the house. Paul has reviewed recent tax appraisal information online, and he believes that $220,000 is a fair price to offer. Paul also does not have a lot of ready cash; so, he is only willing to make a deposit of $2,000 at the time of contracting, and to pay no more than $10,000 in cash at the time of closing. Paul also has told you that he is nervous about whether he will qualify for a loan given his teacher's salary, and he does not want to go through with the deal unless he can obtain conventional bank financing on reasonable terms (not exceeding 6% interest). He would also like sufficient time to look for financing, and prefers that a closing on the house not take place for 90 days. Paul also tells you that he is worried about owing money on both the new house and his current condo. He plans to put the condo on the market right away, but he would like to make the deal for the Laurel Lane house contingent on his selling his current condo.

Your task is to pair with another student to review the form contract and related information that is identified in the **LexisNexis Webcourse** provided for this task. Consider and discuss whether the form contract is a sufficient vehicle to craft an offer on Paul's behalf that addresses his needs, whether an additional clause or clauses are necessary, whether Paul needs to provide you with any additional information, and how you would recommend that Paul complete the contract to submit a written offer to the sellers.

TASK 2:   Assume that Paul approached you regarding the possible home purchase described in Task 1 in the early spring. Given the rash of violent storms that central Minnetoba has experienced in recent years, he expressed concern about the prospect of hail or other storm damage that might occur between the time of contracting and the closing date. Paul wants to make certain that Val and Vernon will be responsible for any loss or damage that might occur during that period. He also told you that he "would like to get out of the deal" if there is some adverse event that causes significant property damage, perhaps exceeding ten percent of the value of the property. You have identified the following "risk of loss" clause in the form contract that Paul previously provided you:

> **17. CASUALTY LOSS:** If any part of the Property is damaged or destroyed by fire or other casualty loss after the effective date of this contract, Seller shall be responsible for restoring the Property to its previous condition as soon as reasonably possible, but in any event by the Closing Date. If Seller fails to do so due to factors beyond Seller's control, Buyer may (a) terminate this contract and the earnest money will be refunded to Buyer, (b) extend the time for performance up to 15 days, and the Closing Date will be extended as necessary, or (c) accept the Property in its damaged condition with an assignment of any insurance proceeds paid or payable to the Seller.

Another clause in the form contract requires the sellers to maintain insurance on the property through the closing date. Your task is to assess whether the above-quoted standard form contract provision will meet Paul's stated wishes on this issue. Review the resources for this Task on the **LexisNexis Webcourse**. If the quoted provision will not meet Paul's wishes, draft a new or revised clause that will meet your client's goals. Then, exchange drafts with a classmate and discuss the approaches that you each undertook.

TASK 3: For purposes of this task, assume that Paul entered into a contract with Val and Vernon for the Laurel Lane house on April 1. Closing is to take place in 90 days. Paul, however, has contacted you again recently concerning the contract. He has decided that he made a big mistake, and he would like to get out of the contract and obtain a return of his earnest money deposit. After several probing questions, you have learned that Paul's girlfriend, Gina, has asked him to move in with her. Paul remembered that the contract included a "subject to financing" clause. It has only been two weeks since he, Val, and Vernon signed the contract, and he promptly applied for a loan at First State Bank of Minnetoba City. Yesterday, however, a bank officer called Paul and told him that his loan application had been denied. Because Paul did not get the loan, he has asked you whether the contract is now "null and void," and he has asked your advice about seeking his deposit back from Val and Vernon. The pertinent portion of the relevant contract clause states the following:

> 12. Buyer shall apply promptly for all financing described below and make every reasonable effort to obtain credit approval for the financing (Credit Approval). Buyer shall furnish all information and documents required by lender for Credit Approval. Credit Approval will be deemed to have been obtained when (1) the terms of the loan described below are available, and (2) lender determines that Buyer has satisfied all of lender's requirements related to Buyer's assets, income, and credit history. If Buyer cannot obtain Credit Approval, Buyer may give written notice to Seller within 60 days after the effective date of this contract and this contract will terminate and the earnest money will be refunded to Buyer. If Buyer does not give such notice within the

time required, this contract will no longer be subject to Credit Approval. Time is of the essence for this paragraph and strict compliance with the time for performance is required.

Agreed Financing:

CONVENTIONAL FINANCING: A mortgage loan in the principal amount of $220,000.00, due in full in 30 years, with fixed interest not to exceed 6 % per annum for the entire loan period.

Buyer hereby authorizes any lender to furnish to the Seller or Buyer or their representatives information relating to the status of Credit Approval of Buyer.

Assume also that the final agreed contract price for the property was $234,000. Paul tendered a $4,000 earnest money deposit at the time of contracting, and the contract requires Paul to provide $10,000 in cash at the closing. Review the e-materials for this task on the **LexisNexis Webcourse** and prepare a list of talking points for a counseling session with Paul. Then, exchange your list with another student and discuss any differences in approach with your classmate.

TASK 4:   In contrast to the facts of Task 3, for purposes of this task assume that Paul would very much like to go through with the deal and close on the Laurel Lane property. Unfortunately, however, he has made extensive efforts to secure conventional financing and has been unsuccessful. Although he has little total debt, the banks have been leery about the size of the loan given Paul's salary level and other assets. Paul called you yesterday and told you about the problem. He also mentioned that he had talked with Val and Vernon and told them about his inability to obtain conventional financing. Paul further told you that the couple remains very motivated to sell the property and that they are willing to agree to amend the contract to provide for seller financing. They are willing to do so on similar terms to the conventional financing terms provided in the contract clause in Task 3. Your task is to review the e-materials for this task on the **LexisNexis Webcourse** and to prepare an initial draft of a modification to the contract that permits seller financing. Identify whether there are any issues or matters for which you need to obtain additional information from your client. Then, exchange drafts with a classmate and compare your approaches.

TASK 5:   For purposes of this task, assume Paul was unsuccessful in his efforts to buy the Laurel Lane house. Val and Vernon accepted a more attractive offer from a different prospective buyer. A few months later, Paul entered into a contract to buy a different house. It is located in the new Pony Pines subdivision in Creek Bay, Minnetoba, which is a small community located near the southern outskirts of Minnetoba City. The house Paul selected is one of six model homes that the developer, Value Homes, Inc., built and furnished as part of the developer's marketing scheme for the development. The house, located at 611 Appaloosa Avenue, is newly constructed and is just to Paul's liking. The contract price was $320,000, and Paul was required to put down a $15,000 deposit as earnest money. The parties entered into the contract on May 1, and the closing is set for July 15. In late April, when Paul toured the 611 Appaloosa property, as well as the other five model homes, a sales representative of Value Homes showed him a large poster that depicted the development plans for the Pony Pines subdivision. It showed a plan for 208 single-family homes, all in a similar size range to the model homes. Paul had previously seen a comparable depiction of the plan on the Value Homes website. At the time Paul entered into the contract with Value Homes, however, only the model homes were complete, and there was construction ongoing on another five houses located near the model homes. In addition, not all of the streets in the planned subdivision had yet been completed. Because Paul is an early riser during the school year and works out of his home as a consultant during the summer and other school vacations, he has a strong desire to live in a quiet neighborhood. Accordingly, the plans for the subdivision were important to him in his decision-making process.

Assume that it is now June 4. Paul has contacted you regarding a problem that has arisen. He saw in yesterday morning's newspaper that Value Homes had appeared before the Creek Bay Planning and Zoning Commission earlier in the week and — in a close vote — received permission to re-plat the Pony Pines subdivision. Under the newly approved, revised plans, only the two-block area including and around the model homes will remain as single-family homes (approximately 32 home lots). The remaining area will now be devoted to duplexes, quad-plexes, and two-story apartment units. As part of Value Home's presentation to the Planning and Zoning Commission, Mary Jones, the President of Value Homes, indicated that the single-family housing plan was being scrapped given both the downturn in the economy and the March decision by the board of regents for Minnetoba State University to build a branch campus in Creek Bay. Because the new campus will be less than a mile from Pony Pines, the re-designed plat and ensuing construction should help satisfy the anticipated increase in housing needs to support the student population.

Paul is furious. After reading the article in yesterday's paper, he gave Mary Jones a call. He asked her why he was not told about Value Homes' plan to ask the Planning and Zoning Commission to re-plat the subdivision when he first looked at the Appaloosa Avenue property or before he and Value Homes entered into the contract for him to purchase the property. Mary told him, "Paul, we were not at liberty to discuss the new plans for several reasons. First, we were still drafting the re-design in late April, and it was not quite complete. In addition, it would have been premature to let you or other members of the general public know about the plans prior to taking the matter to the Planning and Zoning Commission. For one thing, we did not know whether the Commission members would even be inclined to grant the change. We suspected it would likely be a close vote. Accordingly, for political reasons we did not want to reveal the plans publicly until we had gone through the full regulatory process. I am sorry that we could not tell you earlier, but I think you still have selected a great home in what will be a terrific neighborhood."

Paul no longer wants to close on the contract. He has told you that he "wants to get out of the deal" and to get his $15,000 in earnest money back. Paul plans on coming by your office for a meeting tomorrow afternoon. Your task is to review the **LexisNexis Webcourse** materials for this Task and then prepare a list of talking points for your upcoming client conference. Exchange your list with a classmate and discuss the approach that each of you has taken.

EXERCISE 9-2

GENERAL DESCRIPTION OF EXERCISE: Addressing legal questions involving breaches of a contract for the sale of real property.

SKILLS INVOLVED: Fact and case analysis, creative problem solving, preparation for mediation, representing a client at a mediation session, preparation for counseling a client.

PARTICIPANTS NEEDED: These tasks are collaborative. Task 1 requires 5 participants, and Task 2 should include 2 participants.

ESTIMATED TIME REQUIRED:

Task 1: 1.5 hours — 45 minutes to analyze and 45 minutes to mediate

Task 2: One hour — 45 minutes to analyze and 15 minutes to discuss your approach with a classmate

LEVEL OF DIFFICULTY (1-5):

ROLES IN EXERCISE: You are acting as a lawyer for the parties as identified in the various tasks. Some of you will serve as a mediator in Task 1.

THE EXERCISE: 9-2

The following two factual scenarios involve issues pertaining to remedies for breaches of real estate contracts for residential property. Assume that you are a recent graduate of Minnetoba State Law School, and that you have been practicing at a small law firm in Minnetoba City for about a year.

TASK 1: Sara Saylor recently entered into a contract to sell her home at 1717 Sycamore Lane in Minnetoba City, Minnetoba, to Bev Byer. Bev recently graduated from pharmacy school in Calitoba, and has landed a job with the Dandy Drug store in Minnetoba City. She toured Sara's home during a weekend house-hunting trip and fell in love with the house. She offered $300,000 for the house, which Sara accepted. Bev also provided a $40,000 deposit, which was placed in escrow pending the closing. The contract was finalized on June 15, and the closing is set for September 1. Bev was planning to fly over from Calitoba to close on the house that day, and then fly home to move her belongings from Calitoba to Minnetoba City over the Labor Day weekend. Problems arose, however, shortly after the July 4 weekend. Sara and her ex-husband, Howell, were reunited at a family gathering and have decided to reconcile. Howell wants to return to the family home, and Sara has agreed. Accordingly, on July 15 Sara informed Bev that she was not going to go through with the deal, but that she would promptly direct that the deposit be returned.

Bev is very upset. After a shouting match with Sara over the phone, both she and Sara have retained counsel. Upon reviewing the parties' contract, the lawyers for the respective parties have noticed the following dispute resolution provision:

> **16. MEDIATION:** Seller and Buyer agree that before any lawsuit may be undertaken, any dispute between Seller and Buyer related to this contract must first be submitted to a mutually acceptable mediation service or provider, and good faith efforts must be undertaken to resolve the dispute in mediation. The parties to the mediation shall bear the mediation costs equally.

Bev and Sara have now authorized their lawyers to meet with a mediator at the Minnetoba City Dispute Resolution Center to discuss a possible resolution of the current situation. Your professor will assign you to represent Bev or Sara, or to serve as the mediator. Located on the **LexisNexis Webcourse** for this part of the exercise are short videos of client interviews between Bev and Sara and their respective counsel. There is also a link to information for those of you who are designated by your professor to serve as the mediator. After reviewing and considering the linked material for your role, you are to (1) develop your plan and strategy for the mediation session; (2) participate in a mediation — your professor will identify the match-ups for these sessions; and (3) draft a memorandum of agreement if you are able to reach a settlement during the mediation. You are to assume that the mediation is scheduled to take place on August 2, approximately one month prior to the agreed closing date set forth in the contract.

TASK 2: Review and consider the initial facts from Task 1 with regard to the contract between Sara and Bev. For purposes of this task, however, assume that although Sara and Howell reconciled over the July 4 weekend, Sara did not repudiate the contract to sell her home at 1717 Sycamore Lane and is ready and willing to go forward with the deal. In fact, she and Howell have decided to live together in Howell's condo near Lake Minnetoba and to use the sales proceeds for some exotic traveling. This would allow them to have a "fresh start" for their lives together. Unfortunately, on August 1, Bev's job with Dandy Drug fell through. Dandy apparently sold out to a national drugstore chain, and Bev's position was eliminated. Bev decided that without the Dandy Drug job, she could not afford to go through with the purchase of the Sycamore Lane house. Bev still plans to move to Minnetoba, but she is now going to share an apartment with a friend from college while she looks for work. Given the circumstances, she informed Sara that she was not going to go through with the deal, and she asked Sara to return her deposit; however, Sara refused. In addition, after Bev's notice of breach, Sara put the house back on the market. Sara also moved out of the house over the Labor Day weekend and moved in with Howell as planned. Bev has learned that Sara subsequently entered into a new contract with Ned Dorfman on October 1 to sell the house to Ned for $280,000. The closing on the new contract is scheduled for December 1.

Assume that Bev plans to meet with you in the next few days to discuss her options. It is now October 15, and she still has heard nothing further from Sara about the deposit. She would very much like to get her deposit back. You may also assume that Bev has provided you with a copy of the contract for sale that was executed by both Bev and Sara. The contract required that Bev provide $40,000 in escrow as a deposit (identified as "earnest money" in the contract), and stated that the earnest money would be forfeited in the event of Bev's breach. The contract provision did not, however, specifically identify the earnest money as constituting liquidated damages in the event of a breach by Bev. The contract also stated that a prevailing party in any legal proceeding related to the contract may recover reasonable attorney's fees and court costs.

Review the cases and materials on the **LexisNexis Webcourse** for this task, and prepare a list of talking points for your upcoming client meeting with Bev. Then, exchange lists with a classmate and discuss your approaches.

Chapter 10

LAND SALES: MARKETABLE TITLES, DEEDS, AND CLOSINGS

INTRODUCTION

Each party to a land sales contract wants something as a result of entering into the contract. The seller is seeking money and the buyer wants a deed which conveys good title to the property. In this chapter, we focus on how the seller makes the buyer "happy" by providing the buyer with marketable title when contract performance occurs, that is, at the closing. Chapter 9 covers issues surrounding the buyer's performance, such as real estate financing.

Marketable Title

Unless the real estate contract provides otherwise, the seller must provide marketable title or, as it is also called, *merchantable* or *insurable* title. How is the "quality" of a title determined, recognizing that it is not feasible to provide a "perfect" title, as it is impossible to be certain that no title flaws exist? For example, a grantor, many steps back in the chain of title, might have lacked the legal capacity to sign the deed because the grantor was under eighteen years old or have lacked the mental capacity to sign the deed due to the onset of Alzheimer's.

The normal standard for marketable title is that the title is not subject to a reasonable doubt. In other words, a reasonable, prudent, and intelligent purchaser who is guided by competent legal advice would be willing to accept the title to the property and pay fair value for it. Some jurisdictions adopt a slightly different test which may be a bit stricter. The title must be good enough that a court would grant the seller specific performance and thus force an unwilling purchaser to accept the title.

Here is a list of some of the title defects that would render the title not merchantable:

- The seller is unable to convey a fee simple absolute interest in the property.

- The land is burdened by encumbrances such as mortgages, deeds of trust, tax liens, or judgment liens.

- The land is subject to privately imposed restrictions such as easements and covenants.

- There is a break in the chain of title. In other words, the seller cannot show vertical privity between prior owners of the land and the seller.

Buyers will often agree in the sales contract to a title that is not marketable for stated reasons such as the existence of easements or covenants. If the defect was not anticipated, the buyer cannot wait until the time of the closing and use the defect as an excuse to terminate the contract or claim that the seller is in breach. Instead, the buyer must give the seller a reasonable time to correct the defect.

If a title has many potential flaws, the seller can bring a *quiet title* or *trespass to try title* action. All parties with a possible interest in the land are brought together in one lawsuit. Each party presents the evidence supporting a claim to the land. The court will then determine what interest, if any, each party has in the property.

Deed

A deed is the written instrument the owner of an interest in property (the grantor) uses to convey or transfer that interest (or a lesser interest) to a new owner (the grantee). A deed typically consists of the following components:

a. *Premises*

The premises of the deed contains (1) the names of the grantor and the grantee, (2) words of grant such as "I convey" or "I give" which manifest an intent by the grantor to convey an interest to the grantee, (3) a legal description of the land (more on this later in this introduction), (4) the estate granted such as a fee simple or a life estate (see Chapter 7), and (5) the consideration paid. Note, however, that consideration is not necessary for a deed because a deed is not a contract. It is no one's business how much the grantee paid for the property. Nonetheless, a nominal consideration is often stated to help the grantee demonstrate that the transfer was not a gift, thereby giving the grantee a better chance of qualifying as a bona fide purchaser.

b. *Habendum*

The habendum states the limitations on the estate the grantor is conveying if the grantor is not transferring a fee simple absolute.

c. *Reddendum*

Any interest the grantor is retaining in the property, such as an easement, is described in the reddendum.

d. *Warranties of Title*

The grantor's promises regarding the quality of the title and what the grantor will do if the title is not as promised are described in the warranty part of the deed. Title warranties are discussed later in this introduction.

e. *Signatures*

The grantor signs the deed. The grantee does not sign the deed. Remember, a deed is a transfer document, not a contract, and thus is signed only by the person relinquishing an interest in the property.

f. *Acknowledgment or Notarization*

A deed is typically acknowledged in front of a notary. Although this might not be necessary for a valid deed, it is necessary in many states so that the deed may be recorded. See Chapter 11 for a discussion of recording.

The formalities for the execution of a valid deed are relatively straightforward. The common law requirement of a seal is virtually non-existent under modern law. As mentioned above, the grantor signs the deed but the grantee does not. In some states, a deed requires one or more witnesses. After the grantor executes the deed, the deed is acknowledged but, as discussed above, the acknowledgment is to make recording of the deed possible but is not a requirement for its validity. To complete the transfer, the grantor physically delivers the deed to the grantee who then accepts the deed.

At this point, you might wish to perform Task 1 where you will access a deed and attempt to locate the deed elements.

Property Description

A deed must contain an accurate description of the property that the grantor is transferring to the grantee. The description must be sufficient so that a person could locate and identify the land being transferred from all other property. Legal descriptions are more than a mere street address. Property descriptions begin with a survey and are then followed by a description of the land. Three main description systems are in common use in the United States.

a. *Metes and Bounds*

This traditional method of property description which is still in use today, especially in the northeast, describes the perimeter of the property. The description starts at a fixed point which can be located with certainty and then explains how one would travel to enclose the property being conveyed. The beginning and subsequent turning points are called *monuments*. Problems can arise because certain monuments, especially those used in the past such as a tree, fence, stream edge, or boulder, can change in location or be unlocatable over time. In modern times, the monuments are often stakes affixed by the United States Geological Survey. Problems may arise if the description does not *close*, that is, the description does not end where it began. Use of this system is problematic for large tracks of land.

b. *Public Land Survey System*

Because of the problems with the metes and bounds system, the United States government developed a *rectangular survey system*. Land is divided into 36 square mile *townships* which are then divided into square mile *sections* each containing 640 acres.

c. *Lot and Block Survey*

Both the metes and bounds system and the public land survey system are very awkward to use for small parcels of property in urban or other developed areas. To solve this problem, the lots and block survey system developed. The owner of a large tract of property begins by describing the property using whichever of the other two systems is in common use in the owner's area. Then, the owner prepares a detailed map of that area and divides the property into larger blocks and smaller lots with their exact location and dimensions shown on the map. The owner often gives this area a unique name which then becomes the name of development. The owner then records the map in the deed records. Each parcel may now be easily described by block and lots numbers with reference to the plat map.

At this point, you might wish to perform Task 2 where you will access more information about each property description method and determine the type of description method used in the area where you and your family members live.

Methods of Title Assurance

The grantee, especially if the grantee is also a purchaser, should take steps to assure he or she will receive merchantable title. Here are some of the methods the grantee may use.

a. *Personal Covenants of Title*

The grantor may include promises regarding the status of the title in the deed. These promises then protect the buyer against defects in title. However, they rely on the grantor being able to pay damages, and thus, covenants of title should not be the grantee's only method of protection.

1. *Warranty Deed*

A grantor, especially if the grantor is a seller, will typically use a warranty deed to convey the property. A warranty deed traditionally contains six title covenants; three present covenants and three future covenants.

The present covenants of title are breached, if at all, at the moment the grantor delivers the deed. The present covenants include (1) the covenant of seisin (the grantor owns the estate the grantor is transferring and has not previously conveyed it), (2) the covenant of good right to convey (the grantor has the right to transfer the property), and (3) the covenant against encumbrances (the property is free and clear of all encumbrances such as mortgages, easements, and covenants unless the deed is expressly made subject to these encumbrances).

The future covenants of title may be breached in the future when the breach causes actual injury to the grantee. The future covenants include (1) the covenant of quiet enjoyment (the grantee's enjoyment of the property will not be disrupted by the lawful claims of others), (2) the covenant of warranty (the grantor will protect the grantee's quiet enjoyment by defending the grantee's title against the claims of others), and (3) the covenant of further assurance (the grantor will do whatever is reasonably necessary to protect or perfect the grantee's title).

2. *Quit Claim Deed*

A quit claim deed contains no title covenants. The grantor is merely transferring whatever the grantor owns, but the grantor is not promising that the grantor owns anything. In many respects, a quit claim deed is the grantor's release of any claim to the property in favor of the grantee. Many states have statutes that provide that even in the case of a quit claim deed, the grantor is warranting certain basic things such as that the grantor has not previously conveyed the same interest to another person.

3. *Special Warranty Deed*

In a special warranty deed, the grantor makes the standard title covenants but only with respect to actions of the grantor. The grantor does not warrant that the title is clean with respect to events that occurred before the grantor owned the land.

At this point, you might wish to perform Task 3 where you will locate standard warranty and quit claim deed forms for the state in which you intend to practice.

b. *Title Examination*

Instead of relying on warranties and the grantor's credibility and solvency, the grantee may decide to examine the title. If the grantee has the necessary skills, the grantee may search the records. Most grantees, however, lack the skills and resources to conduct a comprehensive title search and thus hire a title company, attorney, or other professional to conduct the search. See Chapter 11 for a discussion of title searching.

c. *Title Insurance*

The grantee, especially if the grantee is a purchaser, will shift the risk of a bad title from both the grantor and grantee to a third party with deep pockets, that is, an insurance company. See Chapter 11 for a discussion of title insurance.

d. *Title Registration*

A few states have adopted the *Torrens* system of title registration which was developed in Australia by Sir Robert Torrens. Title registration begins with a court proceeding, much like a quiet title action, to establish the current condition of the title. The owner then receives a certificate showing the extent of the title and listing all encumbrances such as liens, easements, and covenants. A person claiming an interest that is not listed on the certificate is out of luck unless the claimant can show that the certificate was procured improperly such as by fraud. A prospective grantee need only inspect the certificate to learn all about the property. When the grantor transfers the property, a new certificate is issued. You may notice that, by analogy, this is the way certificates of title for motor vehicles and boats operate.

The Torrens system is used, to some extent, in Colorado, Georgia, Hawaii, Massachusetts, Minnesota, New York, North Carolina, Ohio, and Washington. However, using the system is not required in the vast majority of jurisdictions that authorize its use. Although the system was designed to simplify land transfers, it has not been as popular as anticipated.

At this point, you might wish to perform Task 4 where you will read more about the Torrens system and locate a Torrens certificate.

e. *Adverse Possession*

Adverse possession can be used to bolster a weak or non-existent paper title. See Chapter 11 for a discussion of adverse possession.

Closings

The final step of a real estate sales transaction is the closing, when the buyer pays the agreed consideration (money and/or financing) and the seller delivers the deed to the property. Closings are handled in different ways in different parts of the United States. Closing customs may differ from one area of a state to another. In addition, each real estate sale has unique characteristics which may require variations from the usual custom in the locality.

The closing of most residential real estate sales will be governed by the Real Estate Settlement Procedures Act (RESPA). RESPA is a federal consumer protection statute, first passed in 1974. The purposes of RESPA are to help consumers become better shoppers for settlement services and to eliminate kickbacks and referral fees. RESPA requires that borrowers receive disclosures at various times. Some disclosures spell out the costs associated with the settlement, outline lender servicing and escrow account practices, and describe business relationships between settlement service providers.

At this point, you might wish to perform Task 5 where you will read more about RESPA and conduct a closing.

EXERCISE 10-1

GENERAL DESCRIPTION OF EXERCISE: Study deeds and related documents, conduct a real estate closing.

SKILLS INVOLVED: Document location, examination, and drafting; negotiation.

PARTICIPANTS NEEDED: The first four tasks require one participant. The final task involves six participants.

ESTIMATED TIME REQUIRED:

Task 1: One hour to study a deed and locate all of it major components.

Task 2: 1.5 hours to review detailed information about property descriptions and locate descriptions of specific properties.

Task 3: Two hours to locate statutory and common use deed forms and conduct an analysis of them.

Task 4: One hour to review detailed information about the Torrens system and locate a Torrens certificate.

Task 5: Five hours to prepare for and conduct a closing for a sale of real property.

LEVEL OF DIFFICULTY (1-5):

Tasks 1-4

Task 5

ROLE IN EXERCISE: You are an attorney learning how to conduct real estate transactions. After learning about title assurance, property descriptions, and deeds, you will be involved as the seller, seller's real estate agent, buyer, buyer's real estate agent, lender, or escrow agent in the closing of a residential real estate transaction.

THE EXERCISE

TASK 1: Access the deed of George Strait, the famous country and western singer, which is provided on the **LexisNexis Webcourse** for this Task. Study it carefully and locate all of the components of a typical deed.

TASK 2: Review detailed information about the three property description methods by using the links provided on the **LexisNexis Webcourse** for this Task. Pick four of your relatives or friends who are homeowners. To the extent that you can, pick individuals located in different parts of the country and in different settings (e.g., large metropolitan, suburban, rural). Locate the on-line deed or property records for these properties and analyze the property descriptions. Which method is used in each deed?

TASK 3: The majority of jurisdictions have sample warranty deed and quit claim deed forms in their statutes. Locate the forms for the state in which you intend to practice. Do you think the form is adequate for most clients? Is it too simple or too complex? How would you change the forms in your practice?

Next, locate common use deed forms in the state in which you intend to practice. These are often available from state or local bar associations, state real estate commissions, or commercial publishers. Which one do you like best and why?

TASK 4: Review more detailed information about the Torrens system by using the links provided on the **LexisNexis Webcourse** for this Task. Then, use the internet to locate a Torrens certificate.

TASK 5: Each person selects a role as seller, seller's real estate agent, purchaser, purchaser's real estate agent, lender, or escrow agent (attorney or title company closer). The purchaser locates real estate listings (e.g., the local newspaper, real estate booklets printed by real estate companies which are often found near the entrances to stores, especially large supermarkets, and the internet). The purchaser then selects a home and negotiates with the seller about the terms of the sale, and they enter into a real estate sales contract working with the escrow agent as appropriate. The buyer negotiates the terms of the mortgage or deed of trust with the lender. Thereafter, the escrow agent conducts the closing of the sale in full compliance with RESPA.

This task is purposely left unstructured to make it as realistic as possible. Everyone must work together to construct a transaction that is fair to all parties. Although you may not be able actually to perform each real-life step, be sure to make notes of those steps and how you would accomplish them. The **LexisNexis Webcourse** for this Task has links to materials which you should study and explore carefully before starting this task. Be sure to follow the applicable links from these pages as well. You may also find helpful information in Gerry W. Beyer, *Real Estate Transactions — Residential* chs. 17 & 18 (19 West's Legal Forms 4th ed. 2008 and most recent supplement). You are encouraged to search the internet for additional materials which will help you in whatever role you are playing in this task.

Chapter 11

TITLE ASSURANCE — RECORDING SYSTEMS/ADVERSE POSSESSION

INTRODUCTION

In Chapter 9, we addressed issues pertaining to land sales transactions. Then, in Chapter 10, we covered topics relating to marketable title, real estate closings, and deeds. This chapter will focus on problems pertaining to title assurance in real estate transactions, as well as adverse possession issues.

In your Property class, you will no doubt study a number of different issues relating to title assurance. A typical purchaser of real property no doubt wishes to acquire a good title to the property. There might be encumbrances on the title such as liens, easements, and covenants, and the purchaser will desire to be made aware of any such encumbrance. The usual methods of title assurance include deed covenants from the seller to the purchaser (as discussed in Chapter 10), a title opinion based on a review and search of the public deed records, or title insurance to insure the purchaser's title.

Recording Systems.

Records pertaining to land transactions are typically filed in county deed records offices — sometimes called the "recorder's office," the "recording office," or the "registry of deeds." State statutes identify the types of documents that can be recorded in the public records, and these often include deeds, mortgages, deeds of trusts, liens, leases, wills or affidavits of heirship, and other documents pertaining to interests in real property. Usually, public recording of these documents is not necessary for the validity of the instruments between the parties to the transaction. On the other hand, recording is usually critical to establishing a public record of the transaction and to protect a good faith purchaser for value or a lien creditor from competing claims by others — particularly with respect to assertions of prior unrecorded interests.

These vast numbers of filed documents need to be organized to allow review and searching. A small minority of states have *tract indexes*, by which documents are indexed for each identified parcel or *tract* of land in the county. Most states, however, have *grantor-grantee indexes*, by which separate indexes are maintained for grantors and grantees. Accordingly, each record is indexed and organized in two places — first, under the grantor's last name, but also under the grantee's last name. These indexes can then be searched to create a chain of title for a parcel of property. Typically, the prospective purchaser will start by searching the grantee index to locate when, how, and from whom the prospective seller of the parcel acquired title. (The prospective seller of the property will have been the grantee of the transaction in which he or she acquired title.) After locating the deed, the searcher will then be able to identify the prospective seller's grantor, and the process can be repeated back through time to identify the prior grantors of the particular parcel. This chain of title can then be established back to the sovereign or to some more recent time if allowed by the jurisdiction. (Local law or custom might dictate that reasonable searches only go back, *e.g.*, 40, 50, or 60 years.) After establishing the chain of title, the title searcher will then review the grantor indexes to ascertain whether any of the grantors transferred out interests to other third parties that are not a part of the chain of title. If any recorded documents are located, the searcher will then review the documents to evaluate whether they impact the prospective seller's title.

With the exponential changes in information technology over the last several decades, in many ways the traditional grantor-grantee indexes are less efficient and even anachronistic. Many public records offices have begun to create computerized indexes for newer filings. Some others have endeavored to scan older records going back many years. Although a number of jurisdictions now have computerized systems in place to conduct deed searches, these often only go back 30 or 40 years, but not further. For those counties that have extensive computerized records, some offer free web-based searching opportunities, while others require paid subscriptions or limit computer searching to terminals located in the county offices. A significant majority of jurisdictions, however, continue to adhere to their traditional filing systems. A title searcher must, accordingly, still be familiar with the traditional grantor-grantee index system.

Suppose that an owner of real property sells the same land twice to two different people — to A and then B. Who should be entitled to the land? Under the common law approach, the person who was first in time — A — would prevail. State legislatures have enacted recording statutes, however, to protect *subsequent bona fide purchasers for value*. These recording statutes are intended to protect innocent buyers from adverse claims that are unknown and have not been recorded. There are three major types of recording statutes around the country: (1) *race*, (2) *notice*, and (3) *race-notice*.

Race Statutes.

Under a race statute, the purchaser who records first (and thereby *wins* the race to the courthouse), will prevail over another purchaser regardless of whether the prevailing purchaser had notice of the other transaction. Only a few states have adopted race statutes.

Notice Statutes.

Under a notice statute, a subsequent bona fide purchaser for value will prevail over a prior interest if that purchaser takes without notice of the prior interest. The notice can be either actual notice, constructive notice through proper recording in the deed records, or inquiry notice. (As one example of the latter, suppose that O has sold the property to B. However, O previously sold the property to A and A is living on the property. Even if A has not recorded her deed from O, B would be on *inquiry* notice because a reasonable person would inquire as to why A is on the land, and not O.) Roughly half the states have enacted notice statutes. Note that to prevail over a prior interest, the purchaser need not have recorded to have priority, but the purchaser *should* record to be able to enjoy priority over any other subsequent purchaser for value.

Race-Notice Statutes.

Under a race-notice statute, a subsequent bona fide purchaser for value will prevail over a prior interest if that purchaser takes without notice of the prior interest *and* records first. Accordingly, to prevail, the subsequent purchaser for value must *both* take without notice of the prior interest *and* record first. Roughly half the states have enacted race-notice statutes.

Title Insurance.

In addition to deed covenants, most title assurance protection today arises from title insurance. Rather than obtaining a title opinion from a lawyer, a purchaser of real property will buy a title insurance policy to insure against title problems. The title insurance company conducts its own evaluation of the deed records as part of issuing the insurance policy. The typical policy requires the insurer to defend claims that are made against an owner's title and to indemnify the homeowner (insured) for any losses that might arise out of a successful title action by a third party who asserts paramount title to some or all of the property. These policies will ordinarily set forth standard exclusions (for losses caused by such things as zoning ordinances or building codes, or for matters such as boundary disputes that would be revealed by a survey), and might include certain parcel-specific exceptions. An institutional lender will also likely require its own lender's title policy to assure that its mortgage lien has priority over all other liens against the property. Most title insurance companies across the country use standard forms that have been generated by the American Land Title Association.

Adverse Possession.

The public records at times do not reveal certain title problems. For example, if a party acquires a legal interest in land by means of adverse possession, the deed records will likely be silent as to that interest. After all, the owner by adverse possession did not obtain title to the land via a deed or other written instrument. In addition, standard title insurance policies will exclude from coverage claims by persons in possession who are not shown in the public records. Accordingly, it is worthwhile to consider issues pertaining to adverse possession at this point in our discussion. (Some of the major casebooks address adverse possession in a separate chapter or subchapter as an independent topic. Because of the overlap with title assurance, we have opted to include the discussion here.)

An owner of real property has the right to bring an action to eject or oust a non-owner, third party who is in possession of the property. The record owner must do so, however, prior to the running of the state's statute of limitations for an action in ejectment. If the party in possession meets the required elements for adverse possession for the requisite statutory period, that party will be deemed to have acquired the property by *adverse possession*. In effect, the record owner will have lost the right to bring an action to eject the adverse possessor after the running of the statute of limitations and will no longer be deemed to be the owner of the property. These statutes vary in duration from state to state (or even within a state depending on the type of situation), and can be for five, ten, fifteen, or more years.

To obtain ownership to land by adverse possession, the adverse possessor typically must meet the following elements: (1) *actual possession*, which is (2) *exclusive*, (3) *open and notorious*, (4) *adverse or hostile*, and (5) *continuous* for the requisite statutory period. You will no doubt consider and discuss a wide array of sub-issues pertaining to the interpretation of these elements in your Property course, and a detailed discussion is beyond the scope of this brief summary. In practice, these cases tend to be very fact-specific and are usually hotly contested. Although there is some general consistency across the states for most of these legal elements, there is a split of approach on the "adverse or hostile" requirement, and some states expand the element to require that the possession be under a *claim of right*. All states agree that the possession may not be permissive (*e.g.*, a lessee cannot obtain adverse possession), but there is variation beyond that central premise. Some states require the adverse possessor to have a good faith belief that he or she is the true owner of the land. Other states instead require the claimant to demonstrate a form of bad faith intent to dispossess the true owner. (For example, "I know the land is not mine, but I am taking it nonetheless.") A majority of states, however, find the adverse claimant's state of mind to be irrelevant and instead focus on the claimant's acts vis-à-vis the claimed land.

EXERCISE 11-1

GENERAL DESCRIPTION OF EXERCISE: Addressing legal questions involving recording acts and chain of title matters.

SKILLS INVOLVED: Fact analysis and development, utilization of an online deed search database, conducting a deed search in a county deed records office, case research and analysis, preparation for counseling a client

PARTICIPANTS NEEDED: These tasks are collaborative and require two students each.

ESTIMATED TIME REQUIRED:

Task 1: 30 minutes to review and search online information

Task 2: 45 minutes to conduct searches once you travel
to the appropriate county office

Task 3: 45 minutes — 30 minutes to analyze and
15 minutes to discuss with classmate

Task 4: 45 minutes — 30 minutes to analyze and
15 minutes to discuss with classmate

Task 5: One hour — 45 minutes to analyze and
15 minutes to discuss with classmate

LEVEL OF DIFFICULTY (1-5):

ROLES IN EXERCISE: You are acting as either a law clerk or a lawyer for a party as identified in the various tasks.

THE EXERCISE: 11-1

The following factual scenarios involve issues pertaining to real property records and recording acts.

TASK 1:   Assume that you are a law clerk working for an attorney in the Dallas-Fort Worth area of Texas. Cheryl Jones, your boss, has told you that she has a client who is interested in some Tarrant County residential property in the "Cobb's Subdivision" of Fort Worth that is either owned or was once owned by Dean Frank W. Elliott and his wife. (Dean Elliott served at various times as Dean of both Texas Tech Law School and Texas Wesleyan Law School.) Ms. Jones has asked you to utilize Tarrant County's public records website to search for the Elliotts' deed, and — if the Elliotts own or did own the property — to identify:

(a)   the Elliotts' grantor(s),

(b)   their grantor(s)' grantor(s), and

(c)   their grantor(s)' grantor(s)' grantor(s).

A link to this searchable website is located on the **LexisNexis Webcourse** for this task.

(d)   In addition, Ms. Jones has told you that while you are searching in the Tarrant County public records website, she would like you to check for some financial information. Another client has some business with Joe T. Garcia's — a popular and well-known Mexican food establishment in Fort Worth. Ms. Jones has told you that she understands that an institutional lender provided an extension on a note and deed of trust in 2011 that extended the maturity for a debt obligation relating to the property where the eatery is located until 2016. She would like you to locate and make a copy of that instrument — if it exists. (More information to assist you in this task is available on the **LexisNexis Webcourse** for this task.)

We urge you to undertake these tasks with a classmate.

TASK 2:   Your task is to locate the public deed records office in the county in which your law school is located. It is likely located in the courthouse or one of the other public buildings. Then, working with another student, go to that office and research the following questions:

(a)   Locate the deed for your Property professor's home. Write down the volume and page number at which the deed is located. In addition, record the name of your professor's grantor or grantors. If, like most locations, the county uses a grantor/grantee index, you will need your professor's full name to conduct the search. If your county instead uses a tract index, you will need a physical address. It is, of course, possible that your law school is located in a county that has automated its deed records in a manner similar to the county featured in Task 1 above. Regardless, we urge you to make the trip to the courthouse or other public building to review the actual records. (Note that for many counties that have begun to automate their real estate records, only recent records will have been indexed electronically. Correspondingly, newer document filings might *only* be available electronically. However, older filings will likely remain in book form, or perhaps on microfiche.) If your professor objects, you can first gently remind him or her that these are public records! If that approach is not acceptable or advisable, however, select another favorite professor or your Dean! Also, you will want to make certain that your selected professor or Dean is the owner (or co-owner) of the real estate in question, and not a lessee. In the latter case, the deed will be in the name of the lessor or lessors.

(b)   After you have identified the name(s) of your professor's grantor(s), research further back in the chain of title to locate and identify the names of their grantor(s). Write down the volume and page number at which that information is located. Then, attempt to go back one further step in the chain to locate the grantor(s)' grantor(s)' grantor(s).

(c)   As you locate the deeds, review them to identify any restrictive covenants or easements of record. It is also possible, particularly if the real estate is located in a housing subdivision or comparable development, that the deeds will include a cross-reference to another filing in the deed records (by volume and page number) in which the property developer has filed a common set of restrictive covenants applicable to all lots in the subdivision or development. If that is the case, identify the volume and page number for those restrictive covenants, locate them, and review them. Your professor might want your advice as to any limitations on his or her use of the property that are based solely on information in the deed records. (Other sources of limitations on use of the property, of course, include state law, local zoning ordinances, and other city or county ordinances.)

TASK 3:   For purposes of the problems in this task, assume that you are a recently licensed attorney in Minnetoba. About three months ago, your client, Connie Chavez, purchased a one-acre tract of undeveloped property in southeast Minnetoba near Lake Julia. Connie lives in Minnetoba City, which is approximately 180 miles from the Lake Julia property. Connie purchased the property from Olive Ownby, who provided her with a quitclaim deed. Connie promptly mailed her deed with the appropriate recording fee to the Jepson County deed recorder's office, and the instrument was recorded the next day. A problem has arisen, however. Last week Connie, along with an architect, drove to the Lake Julia property. They planned to look over the site to assess the type of vacation cabin that might be most suitable for the property, as well as the best location on the property for building the cabin. While they were on the property, Bob Bass drove up, got out of his car, and angrily confronted Connie and her architect. He demanded to know why they were on *his* land. Connie replied that she owned the land, and had purchased it from Olive three months previously. Bob exclaimed, "I don't know anything about that, but it doesn't make much sense to me. I bought this land, along with the adjoining three acres, from Olive about a year and a half ago, and I have the deed to prove it. I just haven't taken any steps to build anything on it. But, I come out every week or two in the spring and summer to do a bit of fishing." Connie and her architect glumly drove back to Minnetoba City, and she called you to ask for your advice.

(a)   Jepson County utilizes grantor-grantee indexes for their real property records. Assume that in a subsequent search of these Jepson County real property records, you located a special warranty deed from Olive to Bob from approximately 18 months ago by which Olive conveyed four acres of land near Lake Julia to Bob. The legal description of the tract conveyed includes the one-acre parcel that Olive appears to have sold to Connie. Review the Minnetoba statute (identified as Minnetoba Statute I) that is set forth on the **LexisNexis Webcourse** for this task. Assess Connie's rights to the property, if any.

(b)   Review the second statute that is set forth on the **LexisNexis Webcourse** for this task (identified as Minnetoba Statute II). Would your assessment change if this statute had been applicable, rather than the statute that was applicable in subpart (a)?

(c)   Would your answers in (a) and (b) above be different if Bob had never recorded his deed?

(d)   Suppose that Bob in fact did not record his deed when Olive sold him the four acres in his parcel. However, assume that when Connie first contacted you, she had not recorded her deed either. The day after her confrontation with Bob, Bob recorded his deed, and several days later — after talking with you — Connie recorded her deed. What result if Minnetoba Statute I is applicable? What result if Minnetoba Statute II is applicable?

(e)   Suppose that Bob did not record his deed when Olive sold him the four-acre parcel. Then, Connie promptly recorded her deed to the one-acre parcel after her acquisition from Olive. However, suppose that at the time of Connie's purchase, Bob had hired contractors who had begun building a fishing cabin on the one-acre parcel. Although the cabin was not complete, a slab had been poured and the contractors had erected the frame for the building. What result if Minnetoba Statute I is applicable?

(f)   Would your answers in (a) and (b) above have been different had Olive transferred the four acres to Bob by gift, rather than through a sale?

After working through these questions, exchange and discuss your answers with those of a classmate.

TASK 4:

(a)   Refer to the initial facts set forth for Task 3. For purposes of this task, assume, instead, that after Bob acquired the four-acre parcel from Olive, he did not record his deed. Then, assume that six months after he acquired this real property (and about a year before Connie came into the picture), Bob sold the tract to Ann Andrews by a general warranty deed. Ann promptly had her deed from Bob recorded. Although Ann owned the four-acre parcel as of that time, she left it undeveloped. Thereafter, as in Task 3, Connie purchased her one-acre parcel from Olive and had her deed recorded in the Jepson County deed records office. Assume, then, that it was Ann (and not Bob) who encountered and confronted Connie and her architect on their trip to view the

Lake Julia property. In a dispute between Ann and Connie relating to ownership of the one-acre parcel, who should prevail under either Minnetoba Statute I or Minnetoba Statute II? Both of these statutes are available on the **LexisNexis Webcourse** for Task 3.

(b) Suppose that you had been advising Ann at the time she acquired the four-acre tract from Bob. What advice should you provide to her to assure that her interests are protected under the state's recording statute (either Minnetoba Statute I or Minnetoba Statute II)?

Work with another student to analyze and discuss the problems in this task. First, however, you will likely find the materials referenced on the **LexisNexis Webcourse** for this task to be helpful.

TASK 5: As in the last two tasks, assume that Olive sold the four-acre, undeveloped parcel near Lake Julia in Minnetoba to Bob. For purposes of this task, however, assume that the conveyance took place about five years ago. Bob did not record his deed at that time. Then, about a year ago, irritated that Bob had never done anything to develop the land, Olive transferred the same four-acre parcel to her favorite niece, Nancy Norman, by a gift deed. At the time Olive told Nancy, "You know, I sold this property for next to nothing to Bob a number of years ago. He's never done anything with it. What a waste. So, I'm going to give it you. After all, Bob doesn't deserve it anymore." Nancy promptly recorded her deed. A week or so later, she was bragging about now owning the land at the Tip Top Tavern near Lake Julia when Bob happened to walk in and overhear the conversation. Angered, Bob shouted that he owned the land. Nancy told him that Olive had now given her the land, and she exclaimed, "It's all legal because I took my deed down to the courthouse to get it recorded." Bob stormed out of the bar, went home, found his deed, and took it to the courthouse the next day and had his deed recorded. Nothing more happened with the property for some time. Neither Bob nor Nancy consulted an attorney, and neither took steps to develop the property.

Thereafter, for purposes of this task, assume that Nancy (and not Olive) sold the one-acre parcel described in Task 3 to Connie. The transaction took place about a month ago, and Nancy did not tell Connie anything about Bob. Connie had her deed to the one-acre parcel recorded by the Jepson County recorder of deeds. Then, just as in Task 3, assume that Connie, along with her architect, drove to the Lake Julia property. Like in Task 3, they planned to look over the site to assess the type of vacation cabin that might be most suitable for the property, as well as the best location on the property for building the cabin. While they were on the property, Bob drove up, got out of his car, and angrily confronted Connie and the architect. He demanded to know why they were on *his* land. Connie replied that she owned the land, and had purchased it from Nancy about a month previously. Bob exclaimed, "Nancy doesn't have any legitimate rights to this land! I bought it fair and square from Olive, along with the adjoining three acres, about five years ago, and I have the deed to prove it. In fact, it's recorded down at the courthouse. I know that I haven't gotten around to building anything on it, but I come out every week or two in the spring and summer to do a bit of fishing." Connie and her architect glumly drove back to Minnetoba City, and she called you to ask for your advice.

Assume that after Connie's call, you reviewed the Jepson County grantor-grantee indexes. That search revealed the following:

(1) A special warranty deed from Olive to Bob from approximately five years ago by which Olive conveyed four acres of land near Lake Julia to Bob. The legal description of the tract conveyed includes the one-acre parcel that Nancy appears to have sold to Connie. Although the Olive to Bob deed was dated approximately five years ago, it appears to have been recorded about a year ago.

(2) A quitclaim deed from Olive to Nancy for the exact same four-acre parcel that was also described in the Olive to Bob deed. The date on the deed is just over a year ago. It also appears that the deed from Olive to Nancy was recorded exactly eight days prior to the date when the deed from Olive to Bob was recorded.

(3) A quitclaim deed from Nancy to Connie from about a month ago, which appears to have been recorded two days after it was executed.

In a dispute between Connie and Bob regarding the one-acre parcel that Connie purchased from Nancy, who should prevail? Assume that Minnetoba Statute I, as provided in the **LexisNexis Webcourse** for Task 3, is in effect. In addition, the Minnetoba courts follow the case that is identified in the **LexisNexis Webcourse** for this task. Work with another student and analyze the issues involved.

EXERCISE 11-2

GENERAL DESCRIPTION OF EXERCISE: Assessing legal questions involving an adverse possession claim.

SKILLS INVOLVED: Fact and case analysis, preparation of a client letter, and preparing for a client counseling session.

PARTICIPANTS NEEDED: This task is collaborative. Students should work in pairs.

ESTIMATED TIME REQUIRED:

Task 1: 1.5 hours — 60 minutes to analyze and 30 minutes to prepare client letter

LEVEL OF DIFFICULTY (1-5):

ROLES IN EXERCISE: You and a classmate are acting as lawyers for a party as described below.

THE EXERCISE: 11-2

Assume that you and a classmate are recent graduates of Minnetoba State Law School, and that you have been practicing together at a small law firm in Minnetoba City for about a year.

TASK 1:   Your client, Allie Parsons, lives at 1312 Birch Street in Minnetoba City. She purchased her home from Bill and Belinda Boyle eight years ago. Her neighbors to the immediate east of her property are Carl and Corinne Caswell, and their address is 1308 Birch Street. Carl and Corinne, however, have been trying to sell their home for the last few months. They entered into a contract for sale to Dave Dunston about six weeks ago. Then, about a month ago, Corinne told your client that a survey and title search of the property had revealed that there was some sort of problem. Corinne claimed that the survey and deed records showed that the Caswell property line actually extended five feet west of what Allie (and the Caswells) had thought was the boundary line between the two lots. Corinne then told Allie that to assist the Caswells in going through with their sale to Dave, they would need Allie to have her fence and hedges moved at least five feet to the west of their present location. The two lots (1308 Birch and 1312 Birch) are both 120 feet "deep" from north to south. The lots are bound by Birch Street on the north, and a paved alley to the south. Along what both Allie and the Caswells had previously believed to be the property line, there is a wooden fence that is located north to south over the 50 feet nearest the paved alley. The fence then goes directly west another 10 feet to the east edge of Allie's house. Additionally, there is a solid row of hedges that runs along what had been believed to be the property line from the sidewalk abutting Birch Street for 70 feet to the corner of the fence. The hedges are about 6-7 feet high. The following diagram illustrates the location of the various landmarks described above (although it is not drawn entirely to scale):

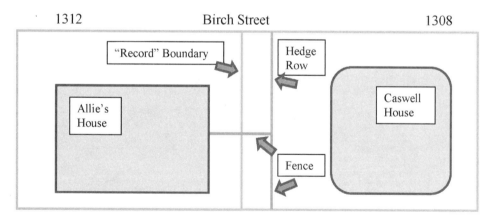

Allie did not do anything in response to her conversation with Corinne because she believed that the information Corinne relayed just had to be wrong. Then, a week ago, Allie received a letter from Lacy Lyles, who is an attorney representing Carl and Corinne. In that letter, Ms. Lyles asserted that Allie is encroaching on the Caswells' property, and she demanded that Allie remove the fence and hedges from the Caswells' property within 30 days or she would file a suit seeking to enjoin Allie from any additional encroachment on the Caswells' land.

Allie then promptly hired you to assist her in this matter. Assume that you thereafter met with Allie in your office a few days ago. In the **LexisNexis Webcourse** materials for this task, you will find a video of that client interview. Your task (working with a classmate) is to view the video and review the statute, cases, and other information for which there are links in the **LexisNexis Webcourse** for this exercise. Then, prepare a letter to Ms. Lyles on behalf of your client stating your client's position about the Caswells' claim. In addition, prepare some notes to assist you in counseling with your client about the strengths and weaknesses of her claim to the disputed property in the event that the Caswells file suit.

By the way, Ms. Lyles' address is:

> Ms. Lacy Lyles
> 1415 N. Main St., Suite 817
> Minnetoba City, Minnetoba 90143.

Chapter 12

EASEMENTS

INTRODUCTION

An easement is the right to use or enjoy another person's property for a limited or specific purpose. Although an easement is an irrevocable property interest, it does not include the right to possess the property. Common examples of easements are a person's use of a road across land the person does not own or the installation of utility lines or pipes (e.g., electric, gas, telephone, cable, water, etc.) over or under the land of others.

When confronted with an easement, it is often helpful to identify three main aspects of the easement.

First, determine the parcels of land involved with the easement. The land burdened by the easement is called the *servient tenement*. It is the land which "suffers" because the easement allows another person to use the owner's property. If it were not for the easement, the owner could prevent the use because the person would be a trespasser. The land, if any, that is benefited by the easement is called the *dominant tenement*. The owner of this parcel of land has the right to use the servient tenement according to the terms of the easement.

Second, determine if the easement holder has either the right to do something on the servient tenement or alternatively has the right to prevent the owner of the servient tenement from doing something on the land. If the easement holder has the right to do something on the burdened land or which impacts the burdened land, the easement is called *affirmative*. Most easements are affirmative, such as the right to use a road. If the easement holder can prevent the owner of the burdened land from doing something on the burdened land, the easement is called *negative*. For example, the easement could prevent the servient tenant from constructing a building which blocks the dominant tenant's view of the ocean or prevents sunlight from reaching the dominant tenant's solar panels.

Third, determine if the easement is connected to the land or to a person. If the easement benefits the dominant tenement regardless of who owns the land, then the easement is called *appurtenant*. The easement *runs with the land* so that whomever owns the dominant tenement may enjoy the benefits of the easement. If instead the easement benefits a person, the easement is *in gross*. For example, a boat owner may obtain an easement from the owner of lakeside property so the boater can launch the boat. If the easement is in gross, there is no dominant tenement, only a dominant tenant. Easements that were in gross were not recognized under common law and even today they are often subject to different rules.

119

There are two interests related to easements. The first is the *profit à pendre* which is often shortened to *profit.* A profit gives the dominant tenant not just the right to use the servient tenement but also the right to remove a portion of the land or its products such as crops, timber, or minerals. At common law, profits had different rules than easements, but under modern law, they are treated similarly.

The third interest is the *license,* also called *an easement at will.* A license is a revocable right to use the land of another such as a ticket to a concert or sporting event. Generally, a license is too "weak" of a property interest to be treated as an interest in land. In many respects, licenses are treated as contracts, so that the rights and remedies of the parties are governed by contract law.

The law recognizes three basic types of easements:

Express easements. An express easement is created with the express intent of the parties by including the appropriate language in a deed. The servient tenant may *grant* the easement to the dominant tenant. Alternatively, the dominant tenant may *reserve* an easement when the dominant tenant sells the servient tenement. Under modern law, the dominant tenant may convey the property *except* for the easement, but at common law, this difference in terminology was significant, with an exception being ineffective. At common law and still in many states today, the grantor of land cannot reserve an easement in favor of a third party. Instead, the grantor must reserve the easement for him- or herself and then expressly grant that easement to the third party.

Implied easements. The court will imply an easement even though the easement is not documented in a deed if the parties intended to grant or reserve an easement. The grantor must have been in a position to have granted or reserved the easement if the grantor had "remembered" to include it in the deed. Accordingly, both the dominant and servient tenements had to be under common ownership at the time of the implied grant or implied reservation. There are two types of implied easements.

The first type of implied easement is the *implied easement by necessity.* This easement arises when the grantor conveys a parcel of property which is landlocked, that is, has no access to a public road. Without an easement, the property would be inaccessible and unusable and thus public policy is in favor of deeming that an easement for access exists. (Note that the law does not consider helicopter or airplane access as removing the necessity.) Traditionally, an implied easement is for physical access, but some courts extend access to include utilities such as electricity, telephone, and water. The implied easement by necessity exists only so long as the necessity exists. Thus, if a public road is later built so the property is no longer landlocked, the easement ends.

The second type of implied easement is the *implied by prior use easement* (also called a *quasi-easement*). A court may be willing to imply the easement if the facts show that the parties intended a use which was ongoing when the property was one parcel to continue after the severance. Courts are reluctant to impose an easement which restricts a property owner's rights unless the evidence is sufficient to justify doing so. Thus, each case is considered on its own merits, and different jurisdictions may require different types or strengths of evidence. The typical types of evidence which can support an implied by prior use easement include (1) the prior use was either apparent or discoverable by reasonable inspection, (2) the prior use was permanent or continuous, and (3) the easement is necessary and beneficial. With regard to this third factor, some courts make a distinction between an implied grant and an implied reservation. Because the grantor wrote the deed and could have easily reserved an easement, the easement may need to be virtually a necessity before a court will hold that it exists. But, if the grantee is claiming an implied grant, a showing that the easement would be helpful or convenient may be sufficient. The court will examine all other relevant evidence such as the price paid for the land (e.g., did the dominant tenant pay more for the land than it was worth if the easement was not included?), whether the easement provides reciprocal benefits (e.g., may each property owner use the same road to cross the other property owner's land?), and, of course, the exact language of the deed (is it written to allow for or preclude the easement?).

Prescriptive easements. The court may determine that an easement exists if the alleged dominant tenant can demonstrate that an easement exists because of long and continued use. Obtaining an easement by prescription is analogous to obtaining ownership of land through adverse possession. There are significant differences among the jurisdictions regarding what the alleged dominant tenant must prove before a court will burden the servient tenement with an easement. Here are the typical elements.

The alleged dominant tenant's use of the property must be open and notorious. In other words, the use must be without the property owner's permission or consent. If the property owner had agreed to the use, the use would then be deemed a license. The alleged dominant tenant's use must be adverse to the owner's claim of right to the property. In other words, the property owner would have had the ability to prevent the use if the owner had so desired. Although an easement is a non-exclusionary interest, a few jurisdictions require that the alleged dominant tenant prove that the use was exclusive, that is, that no other person was using the easement even including, in some states, the landowner. The alleged dominant tenant must also show an uninterrupted use for a sufficiently long period of time, typically ten or more years.

An express easement should carefully describe all aspects of the easement such as its location and exactly how the easement may be used. If issues arise which are not covered by the terms of the easement, the court will apply the *rule of reason* and balance the benefit to the dominant tenant against the burden on the servient tenant. The court will examine all relevant factors including how the property was used before the grant or reservation of the easement, the purpose of the easement, and the amount paid for the easement.

EXERCISE 12-1

GENERAL DESCRIPTION OF EXERCISE: Examine easements contained in deeds, search public records, review tax records.

SKILLS INVOLVED: Fact analysis and development, understanding and identifying potential problems with easements, identifying conflicts between deed restrictions and photographs of the property, drafting a letter to clients.

PARTICIPANTS NEEDED: Only one participant is needed for the following tasks.

ESTIMATED TIME REQUIRED:

Task 1: 30 minutes to view the video-recorded client interview and prepare a file memo.

Task 2: 1 hour to view and carefully study photographs for any potential express or implied easements that may exist.

Task 3: 1.5 hours to access the Travis County Public Records page, perform a "deed search" according to the instructions, and carefully read over all documents that will help you advise your client.

Task 4: 1 hour to access the tax documents for the property and determine if the value of the property will decrease.

Task 5: One hour to review the right-of-way document.

Task 6: Two hours to write a letter to your client specifically detailing your findings.

LEVEL OF DIFFICULTY (1-5):

ROLE IN EXERCISE: You are an attorney specializing in real estate transactions. You will advise a new client regarding the value of a potential purchase of real property.

THE EXERCISE

TASK 1:   Marcus Cain has come to your office in search of advice regarding his purchase of a 50.27 acre plot of land. Mr. Cain has not done extensive research into the purchase and is now worried about the direction the sale is taking. There are some potentially devastating problems with the property regarding implied and express easements which could seriously harm Mr. Cain's intended use of the land.

Review the video-recorded interview between Mr. Cain and yourself which can be found on the **LexisNexis Webcourse** for this Task. Prepare a memo to your file based on the interview outlining what steps you will take for Mr. Cain. The memo should explain any potential problems you see with the sale and whether Mr. Cain understands the issues with the property. Also, make note of the likely existence of any express or implied easements that might pose a problem for Mr. Cain.

TASK 2:   At Mr. Cain's next meeting with you, he shows you several pictures of the property. He had his personal assistant take the pictures. These pictures are available on the **LexisNexis Webcourse** for this Task. Study the pictures carefully to determine if any express or implied easements are likely to exist on the property. Mr. Cain has written notes on the pictures which you will find helpful.

TASK 3:   To learn more about the property, you need to access the online deed records using the following instructions:

1.   Visit the following link: http://deed.co.travis.tx.us

2.   On the left side of the page, click on "Search Official Public Records."

3.   In the field titled "Instrument # From," enter the following number: "2006106888."

4.   Click "Enter."

5.   Click on the first document numbered "2006106888."

   Use the arrows and zoom keys to read the warranty deed. Look for potential issues concerning the property including the existence of express easements or other owners of the property who have not been released.

6.   Click on the "Related Documents" tab.

7.   If there are any other documents that have been filed with the property, you should carefully read them.

8.   Click "Search Results"

9.   Now click on the second result for "2006106888" — a transfer document.

10.   View the transfer document. Read the transfer document carefully, looking for any relevant information to help advise your client.

Note that this deed information is for an existing property different from the one described in Task 1 and shown in the pictures in Task 2. However, for purposes of this activity, you should assume the properties are the same.

TASK 4:   Access the Tax Appraisal information for the property identified in Task 3 by using the following instructions:

1.   Visit the following link: http://traviscad.org.

2.   Click on the "Property Search" link.

3.   Under the heading, "Real Property," click on the "Property ID" link.

4.   Enter the following number: "237051."

Carefully examine the tax appraisal documents to determine the value of the property. Take into special consideration how the discovered easements, which have apparently not been revealed to the appraiser, may adversely affect the value of the land.

Note that this tax information is for an existing property different from the one described in Task 1 and shown in the pictures in Task 2. However, for purposes of this activity, you should assume the properties are the same.

TASK 5:   While you have been poring through Mr. Cain's materials, you had your paralegal do some hunting for any type of easement on the property as you had a nagging doubt that you might have missed something when you searched the records. Your paralegal has returned with a Right-of-Way pertaining to the land in question which is available on the **LexisNexis Webcourse** for this Task. You may assume that the document is properly signed, stamped, and filed. Study this document carefully and make a list of facts and issues that you believe are important.

TASK 6:   Write a memo to Mr. Cain detailing your findings from Tasks 2-5. Include whether you have found any express or implied easements and how those will affect Mr. Cain's use of the land. Also, include your opinion regarding the purchase and the best counteroffer Mr. Cain should make to the seller. Include a request for other information you would like from Mr. Cain that would help you represent his interests more completely.

Chapter 13

COVENANTS AND SERVITUDES

INTRODUCTION

A *real covenant* is a contract which is enforceable not just by the original parties to the contract, but also by successors in interest to these parties because they are now the new owners of the burdened or benefited land. The real covenant binds future landowners even if they do not consent, because the covenant runs with the land.

The requirements of a real covenant evolved out of common law, which was a time when courts disfavored privately imposed restrictions on land use. Accordingly, the requirements for a contract to qualify as a real covenant were originally very strict. These requirements are typically loosened today by courts or legislatures, with jurisdictions often taking significantly different approaches.

The main requirements of a real covenant are:

1. Enforceable promises.

The promises must be enforceable under applicable contract law. For example, the original parties were competent, an offer and acceptance occurred, consideration supported the promises, any applicable requirement for the promises to be in writing was satisfied, and the contract has a legal purpose and does not violate any state or federal constitutional provisions.

2. Intent for the promise to run with the land.

The original parties must have had the intent for their promises to bind not just themselves but instead to run with the land. In other words, the promises were not to be personal to the parties — a party would be benefited or burdened only for so long as the party owned the property connected with the covenant. At common law, special terminology in the grant of the covenant was often needed such as the phrase "and his or her assigns." Under modern law, however, special terminology is not needed as long as it is clear that the promise is to run with or be appurtenant to the land. Nonetheless, it is common to see the term assigns used in grants of real covenants.

3. The promise must touch and concern the land.

For a contract to become a real covenant, it must obviously have a connection to the land. Originally, both the benefit of the covenant and the burden of the covenant had to touch and concern land. A burden touches the land when the burden is something that can only be done by the owner of the servient property. The burden reduces the value of the property but does not restrict the property owner personally.

For a simple example, assume I own land next to yours and make the following promise, "I promise never to build a liquor store on my property and I promise never to drink liquor." The restriction on building a liquor store burdens the land but the promise not to drink only burdens me personally.

A benefit touches and concerns land when it makes the land more valuable by increasing the landowner's use or enjoyment of the land. The benefit does not make the landowner more valuable. For example, if I promise to maintain the fence between our adjoining properties, the promise benefits your land rather than you personally.

As mentioned above, the traditional approach is that both the burden and benefit of a real covenant must touch and concern land. Under modern law, it may be sufficient if just the burden or just the benefit touches and concerns land. In other words, a covenant, like an easement, might be in gross rather than appurtenant.

4. Privity.

At common law, the original parties to a real covenant were required to be in mutual privity of estate, meaning that they each were required to have a simultaneous interest in the same land. This effectively limited real covenants to the landlord-tenant context because a lessor and a lessee have an interest in the same land, but purchasers from a common seller or mere neighbors lack a simultaneous interest in each other's land.

As the law developed, horizontal estate privity was deemed sufficient, that is, as long as the original parties had a special relationship with respect to the land such as being in a buyer-seller or grantor-grantee relationship, the necessary connection existed. This opened up the availability of real covenants to be used in housing developments, as a seller could impose the covenants on all of the lots sold to the various purchasers. However, neighbors were still unable to enter into real covenants because they lacked any type of connection to the same property. They could, however, engage in a straw-person transaction where each would convey the property to a third party who would then impose the covenant on the properties and convey the parcels back to the original owners.

The modern approach is to forgo the necessity of any type of estate privity between the contracting parties. Instead, it is sufficient if the original parties had contractual privity with each other.

Regardless of the approach adopted by a jurisdiction, vertical privity between an original contracting party and the party seeking to enforce a covenant must exist. In other words, the new owner of the burdened or benefited property must be able to trace ownership back to the original party who entered into the covenant.

Because the common law requirements for a real covenant were difficult to satisfy, the courts developed the concept of an *equitable servitude* to deal with situations where it was unfair to excuse a new landowner from complying with the terms of a covenant entered into by a prior owner of the land. For example, in the famous 1848 English case of *Tulk v. Moxhay*, which likely appears in your property casebook, the court relaxed the mutual privity requirement because the purchaser of the property had notice of a restrictive covenant when he purchased the land. The court explained that it would be inequitable to permit a purchaser to have full knowledge of a restriction and then be able to circumvent it merely because the mutual privity requirement for a real covenant was lacking.

The law of equitable servitudes varies significantly among the jurisdictions today. Some courts will permit the purchaser's notice to substitute for other missing elements of a real covenant, while other courts will not.

Some jurisdictions also recognize *implied reciprocal equitable servitudes*, which relax the requirements for enforcement even further. The situation where a court may impose these servitudes is where a seller of lots in a residential subdivision imposes covenants on some, but not all, of the lots, typically because of carelessness in preparation of the description of the covered property in the covenant declaration or deeds. The court may find that because the person purchased a lot surrounded by lots with restrictions, the purchaser was on inquiry notice that restrictions exist because of the obvious uniformity of construction and use of the surrounding lots. This concept is often controversial, because the purchaser may end up being bound by covenants as to which the purchaser has no actual notice (covenants not stated in the purchaser's deed) and no constructive notice (covenants not recorded in the purchaser's chain of title). Nonetheless, some courts find that it is equitable to impose the restrictions because the purchaser should have seen the condition of the surrounding property and exercised due diligence to investigate.

EXERCISE 13-1

GENERAL DESCRIPTION OF EXERCISE: Examine covenants and restrictions contained in a deed, as well as Homeowner's Association bylaws, to determine if any issues exist with a couple's pending purchase of a new home.

SKILLS INVOLVED: Fact analysis and development, understanding and identifying potential problems with real covenants, identifying conflicts between real covenants and photographs of the property, drafting a letter to clients.

PARTICIPANTS NEEDED: Only one participant is needed for the following tasks.

ESTIMATED TIME REQUIRED:

Task 1: 1 hr and 30 minutes to assess facts, carefully read over the deed provided and identify any potential conflicts

Task 2: 1 hour to access the website, read bylaws and deed restrictions, and identify potential conflicts

Task 3: 1 hour to 1 hour and thirty minutes to carefully look over photographs and identify any potential conflicts with the issues you have previously identified in the deed and bylaws

Task 4: 1 hour to draft a letter to your client outlining your findings

LEVEL OF DIFFICULTY (1-5):

ROLE IN EXERCISE: You will act as the attorney for Jerry Jones. Jerry and his wife are purchasing a home in the Ruby Slippers Community in South Texas.

THE EXERCISE

TASK 1: Jerry and Patty Jones, retired entrepreneurs, are purchasing a home in the Ruby Slippers Community in South Texas. Mr. Jones owns The Renegades, a professional basketball team, and his wife Patty makes children's clothing and accessories, which she sells out of their home. Patty plans to continue making and selling children's clothes out of the new home.

The 2,800 square foot, single story house has three bedrooms, two bathrooms, and a large game room that was once a two-car garage. The home has a two-car carport extending from the side of the house, a perfectly manicured front yard, and a large, open backyard. The backyard houses a small storage barn and a ten-foot by ten-foot enclosed garden that backs up to the edge of their property line. Patty intends to remove the garden before they move in. Patty also has plans to build a large, luxury dog house and kennels for the couple's three hunting dogs.

Jerry and Patty have every intention of making this home their primary and permanent place of residence; however, their only daughter's boyfriend has recently requested her hand in marriage, and this house just might be a perfect wedding present. The transfer is not set in stone but the possibility is certainly there.

Jerry would like you to go over the deed before he finalizes his purchase. Read the deed, which can be found on the **LexisNexis Webcourse** for this Task, looking for any facial deficiencies, as well as any provisions that might potentially affect Jerry and Patty's future use of the property.

TASK 2: Jerry is also concerned about the restrictions on the property. Access the Ruby Slippers Homeowners Association website to read the bylaws and deed restrictions. Although the website is for an existing homeowners association not connected to the property described in this problem, please assume that all material on the website applies to this task. Use the following directions:

1. Go to http://www.rubyranchtx.com.

2. To access the Homeowners Association Bylaws, click on the "Bylaws" link on the right side of the page.

3. To access the Homeowners Association Deed Restrictions, click on the "Deed Restrictions" link on the right side of the page. You will be using the "Phase-7-Restrictions" for this task.

4. Use the other links to navigate around the website as you see fit.

You will need to pay specific attention to the bylaws and deed restrictions depicted on the website. Look for any provisions that may already have been violated.

TASK 3: Language in the deed has led Jerry to believe that the property is in violation of the Ruby Slippers Homeowners Association bylaws, as well as restrictions included in the deed. Because neither Jerry nor Patty has the time or knowledge to go over potential problems, they need you to identify any issues.

Jerry and Patty have brought along a few pictures of the property to help you get started. These pictures are included on the **LexisNexis Webcourse** for this Task.

Review these pictures and then examine the covenants contained in the deed as well as the Homeowners Association bylaws referenced in Task 2. Determine if the property "as-is" already violates any of the covenants. Note that these pictures are not from the same home. Do not worry that they do not completely match; you are simply concerned whether each photo meets the deed restrictions.

TASK 4:   Draft a memo to Jerry and Patty detailing your findings. Include the following key points in your memo: (1) any facial deficiencies or potential issues with the way the deed is worded; (2) any deed restrictions that could potentially affect Jerry and Patty's future use of the property; (3) any restrictions set out by the Homeowner's Association that have, or may have, already been violated; and (4) ways that Jerry and Patty may correct any possible violations. Include your professional opinion regarding whether they should go through with the sale and any changes you believe should be made to the deed and the property if they decide to purchase the property.

Chapter 14

GOVERNMENTAL INTERFERENCE WITH PROPERTY RIGHTS

INTRODUCTION

Restraints on land use may be made by the consent of private parties, judicially imposed by the courts, or imposed by legislatures and administrative agencies. This chapter focuses on the last of these restraints, those created by legislatures and administrative agencies. These types of restraints are becoming more common than privately imposed restrictions and may be imposed by all levels of government, although local restrictions are the most common.

The issue presented by legislative and administrative restrictions is determining whether the public interest justifies restricting a person's use of his or her property. This question is answered by balancing the public's right (the good of the many) against the individual's right to use their private property as the person sees fit (the needs of the one).

Types of legislative and administrative restrictions — Generally.

Legislatures and administrative agencies use a variety of techniques to regulate land use. The six most common techniques are as follows:

1. Direct Prohibition or Regulation of Specified Uses.

Certain uses are strictly forbidden on the ground that they are considered serious threats to the public health, safety, or societal morals. Unless expressly allowed under local law, some examples are houses of prostitution and rendering plants (businesses that melt animal fat). Although the prohibited types of activities would probably constitute traditional nuisances, it is broader and easier to enforce an overall restriction than to maintain multiple nuisance actions.

2. Building Codes and Development Permits.

Structures must meet certain building standards. Codes are often very extensive and occupy hundreds of pages of regulations detailing parameters for practically everything. Examples of codes include fire, housing, and health and safety.

3. Zoning.

A community is divided into districts and within each district certain uses are allowed and others are prohibited. We will look at zoning in more detail later in this chapter.

4. Subdivision Regulation.

A local government sets out rules for subdivision of land. Before an owner may subdivide land for development, the way in which the land will be subdivided must be approved by local officials. Subdivision regulation works with zoning to make sure the different pieces of land within a zone fit together. Some examples include streets that line up, sewer and water lines that match, and that there is appropriate drainage of surface water.

5. Reservation of Land for Public Acquisition.

Via the use of official maps, governments indicate where, in the future, schools, roads, and other public areas will be located. Although this property is not yet taken by the government, its future use is restricted. By prohibiting structures from being built on this land, it will be considerably cheaper for the government to obtain it later via eminent domain. The government does, however, get to continue receiving property taxes until it actually takes the property.

6. Public Ownership and Development of Land.

The government simply acquires the land. This can be done by purchase from individuals willing to sell or by eminent domain from individuals unwilling to sell.

Landowner's responses to governmentally imposed restrictions.

The first claim a landowner can make is for a deprivation of due process and equal protection under the Fourteenth Amendment to the United States Constitution. These claims are unlikely to succeed; regulation is permitted as long as the legislative body had a rational basis for the restriction. Just because the value of the land is greatly reduced does not necessarily mean the regulation is unreasonable or arbitrary.

The second claim a landowner can make is a demand for just compensation under the Fifth Amendment. The Fifth Amendment states that "private property [shall not] be taken for public use, without just compensation." The major issue in these situations is determining whether a "taking" has occurred. Courts have held that certain regulations can be a taking just as much as physically taking the land or using government land to the detriment of surrounding land. This is one of the most litigated areas of land use restrictions and will be explored later in this chapter.

Zoning.

The basic idea of zoning is to divide a community into districts with certain land uses allowed and others prohibited in each district. There are several elements of a zoning plan. The most important are discussed below.

1. *Zoning Ordinance.* An ordinance specifying the regulations for each zone.

2. *Zoning Map.* A map showing the zone in which each parcel of land within the community is located.

3. *Differences Between, Consistency Within.* Different zones will have different characteristics, but within each zone, the applicable restrictions are usually uniform.

4. *Types of Zones.*

    a. Use Districts. Restrictions on how the property is used. The most common types of use districts are residential, commercial, industrial, and agricultural.

    b. Height Districts. Regulation of building height.

    c. Land Coverage or Bulk Districts. Examples of types of things regulated include minimum floor space, minimum lot size, specified floor-area ratio, minimum set back distances (how far the buildings must be from the lot line), and minimum open space (amount of the lot not covered by buildings).

    d. Floating Zones. The zoning ordinance permits a certain use but does not identify where on the zoned property the use is allowed. A person wanting to make such a use applies for permission with respect to a specified area.

    e. Holding Zones. In these zones, practically no use of the land is allowed until a later time when the government is able to determine how that land should be used.

5. *Common Characteristics of a Zoning Plan.*

    a. Cumulative Uses. Uses are ranked so that higher ranked uses are permitted in lower ranked areas. For example, single family housing would be permitted on land zoned for business but not vice versa.

    b. Noncumulative or Exclusive. Only the specified use is allowed in each zone.

    c. Conditional Use; Special Exceptions; Special Use. A use which is not expressly allowed or disallowed. The landowner must obtain a special permit following a discretionary review of the use.

    d. Non-Conforming Prior Uses. Although retroactive effect may be given to zoning rules, such effect could be deemed a taking in some situations so that compensation would be required. Thus, zoning ordinances typically allow prior non-conforming uses and structures to remain, that is, to be "grandfathered."

6. *Relief from Zoning Plan.*

    a. Variances. The zoning board often has authority to grant a variance if the property owner can show a good reason such as an unfair hardship or that the non-conforming use will not hurt the surrounding land.

    b.   Amendments — Rezoning. The local legislative or administrative body may amend the zoning regulations to rezone the area so the property owner's desired use is allowed.

7.   *Zoning for Esthetic Purposes.* The contemporary view is that regulations to preserve the esthetic beauty of an area are allowed. However, there may be difficulty with determining whether a violation has occurred, as beauty is in the eye of the beholder.

8.   *First Amendment and Zoning.* Some regulation of billboards and signs, such as size and location, may be allowed. However, claims are often made that these infringe on freedom of speech.

Public Ownership of Land.

If the government still owns land that was never transferred to private hands, it is easy for the government to regulate it. However, there may be an issue if the government acquires private land. The government can purchase private land or take the land using eminent domain. If the owner of the land is willing to sell, then the government may regulate that land as it sees fit. However, if the government takes the property by eminent domain, the government must (1) pay just compensation and (2) use the land consistently with the "public use" requirement of the Fifth Amendment.

One of the frequently litigated issues is whether there is a sufficient public use if, after taking the land, the government imposes restrictive covenants and then sells the land to a private buyer. There are two well-known cases in which the United States Supreme Court has dealt with this issue of whether there was a sufficient public use of the land to justify a taking under the Fifth Amendment.

Hawaii Housing Authority v. Midkiff, 1984. Due to the fact that a large amount of the land in Hawaii was owned by a small number of individuals (47% by 72 individuals), the Hawaii legislature passed a law whereby the government took land by eminent domain from the owners of the property who were renting their property to others, paid "just" compensation, and then transferred the land in fee simple to the individuals who had been leasing the land from the property owners. Some of the landowners objected to the forced sale of their land and brought suit to have the law declared unconstitutional.

The Court noted that the government cannot take one person's property for the benefit of another, even if just compensation is paid, unless there is a public purpose. However, this public purpose may be obtained through the use of a private entity and thus there is no requirement that the government retain possession of the land. The Court stated that it would not substitute its judgment for the legislature's as to what is a public use unless the legislature acted without reasonable foundation. Finding that the law satisfied this standard, the Court upheld the constitutionality of the Hawaii statute.

Kelo v. City of New London, Conn., 2005. The city forced landowners to give up their land by paying just compensation. The land was to be used for private business development which was supposed to benefit the city by creating jobs, generating tax revenue, and building momentum for the city's revitalization. In a 5 to 4 opinion, the Court expanded *Midkiff* and held that the land was taken for a public use. The Court noted that economic development is a traditional function of the government and once again stated that the Court will give great deference to a legislative determination of what constitutes a public purpose. The dissent argued that there is a difference between "public use" and "public purpose" and that a public use did not exist just because the public might benefit from the new use of the land.

This decision caused a huge public outcry, because it permitted the government to take land by eminent domain and then use it for private businesses as long as there was some public benefit achieved. Over 40 states have enacted legislation which to some extent limits *Kelo*-type takings, with approximately 20 states enacting statutes imposing significant limitations.

Regulatory takings.

The Fifth Amendment states that private property shall not be taken for public use without just compensation. What exactly is "taking"? If the government physically occupies the property or the government's conduct results in a deprivation of the person's property, then a taking has occurred and just compensation must be provided. Alternatively, if a government regulation causes a decrease in the property's value, the property owner may claim that a regulatory taking has occurred and just compensation must be provided.

To determine if a regulatory taking has occurred, it first must be determined whether the regulation involves a public use or benefit. If there is no public use or benefit, the regulation is invalid even if there is only a slight change in value. Assuming a public use or benefit exists, it must next be determined whether the regulation is a mere exercise of police power or a taking. A mere exercise of police power (e.g., zoning) is valid and does not require compensation for the decrease in value to the property. It is difficult to draw the line between what constitutes a taking and what is a mere exercise of police power. The following are a few of the key United States Supreme Court cases addressing this issue.

Loretto v. Teleprompter Manhattan Corp, 1982. A New York law required landlords to permit a cable television company to install its cable boxes and wires on the property. A landlord brought suit claiming that this law constituted a taking. The Supreme Court held that permanent physical occupation is always a taking. It does not matter that a public interest is served, that the cable box only occupied a small amount of space, or that there was no significant burden imposed. The dissent noted that the facts of this case were trivial and that this holding would open the floodgates for takings whenever a landlord must physically attach something to the land.

Lucas v. South Carolina Coastal Council, 1992. After the landowner had purchased two residential lots on a South Carolina barrier island with the intent to build single family residential homes on the land, the state enacted the Beachfront Management Act which barred the building of any permanent structures on the land. The Court first noted two situations where a taking automatically occurs without any consideration of the weight of the public purpose supporting the regulation. These automatic takings occur when there is a physical invasion of the property or when the regulation denies the owner of all economically beneficial or productive use of the land.

Because the landowner was deprived of all economically beneficial or productive use of the land, the Court held that a taking occurred and that the Act was not a valid exercise of police powers. The court also explained that there was no exception to these automatic takings unless the law regulates a harmful or noxious use of the property and the state's nuisance law (or other law) would already have denied the landowner all economic use of the property.

Tahoe-Sierra Preservation Council v. Tahoe Regional Planning Agency, 2002. The United States Supreme Court was faced with the issue of whether a regulation that temporarily prohibits all development of a property constitutes a regulatory taking. In this case, property owners were not permitted to develop their land for 32 months while a planning agency worked out a plan for the land. The court held that this was not a per se taking, but that a temporary moratoria on development could be a taking in different circumstances.

Exactions.

Can the government demand something in exchange for allowing a property owner to use his or her property as he or she desires? In the 5-4 decision of *Nollan v. California Coastal Commission, 1987*, the United States Supreme Court held that a taking had occurred when the California Coastal Commission refused to grant Nollan a building permit unless he granted a public easement to use the area between the mean high tide line and his seawall. The court found no nexus between the condition (granting the easement to the public) and the original purpose of the building restriction on the land (protecting the public's ability to see the beach). The government was attempting to further a valid governmental purpose without paying for it. This condition did not substantially advance a legitimate state interest and therefore went beyond mere police power. If the government wants an easement, they must pay for it. In the later case of *Dolan v. City of Tigard, 1994*, the Court held that an exaction is legitimate only if the public benefit from the exaction is roughly proportional to the burden imposed on the public by allowing the proposed land use.

EXERCISE 14-1

GENERAL DESCRIPTION OF EXERCISE: Watch a client interview and review a zoning map, application, and variance application to determine the rights of a new land owner against a future request for a zoning change by a city; determine the rights of a private citizen and the state and federal government when the government attempts to take property by eminent domain.

SKILLS INVOLVED: Fact analysis and development, understanding and identifying potential problems with government interference by zoning changes and eminent domain takings; critical thinking and reasoning from varying perspectives; drafting client letters.

PARTICIPANTS NEEDED: Only one participant is needed for the following tasks.

ESTIMATED TIME REQUIRED:

Task 1: 30 minutes to review a video of a client interview, take notes, and think critically.

Task 2: 2 hours to review zoning maps and ordinances for the property and draft a letter to your client.

Task 3: 2 hours to review a city plan to build a new baseball stadium, conduct research, and draft a letter to your client.

Task 4: 1.5 hours to review a state park proposal to take property by eminent domain and draft a memo.

LEVEL OF DIFFICULTY (1-5):

ROLE IN EXERCISE: You will act as an advising attorney under stated circumstances with various clients.

THE EXERCISE

TASK 1:   You will watch a brief video of an interview with your client regarding his potential purchase of a parcel of land bordering a horse ranch. The interview is found on the **LexisNexis Webcourse** for this Task. Your client plans to use the land for his home as well as for a small horse farm. The city government has recently applied to rezone a large portion of the land and surrounding properties for commercial purposes. Your client is concerned about the future of his purchase and would like to fight the zoning ordinance, if possible. Make sure to take careful notes from the interview to use during the next task.

TASK 2:   Your client from Task 1 has brought you a map of the property, as well as surrounding properties, which includes the various zones in the area. The map is found on the **LexisNexis Webcourse** for this Task. The property at issue is located in the southwest section of the map and is currently zoned for agricultural purposes.

You have also had your legal assistant locate the city's general application for rezoning (the questionnaire) and the application for a variance. These materials are also found on the **LexisNexis Webcourse** for this Task. Use your knowledge from the interview, map, questionnaire, and variance application to draft a letter advising your client whether he should continue with the purchase of the property and the client's chances of preventing the zoning change from going through.

TASK 3:   A potential client, Casey, has entered your office with a fairly vexing problem. She and almost fifty other homeowners in her area have received "buy-out" notices. The notice from Mr. James, the owner of the area's professional baseball team, states that he will pay 25% above market value for their homes. Casey does not want to sell and declined the offer when it was initially received about a month ago. However, Casey has now received a notice from the Attorney General of the State of X condemning her house. This notice also states that Casey will be paid a reasonable amount for the taking of her home, a number which is substantially lower than Mr. James' initial offer.

After researching the requirements of a successful eminent domain taking, draft a letter to Casey advising her of her potential options, including accepting the original offer by Mr. James, which, according to the team's owner, remains open for ten more days despite the Attorney General notice.

Then, assume that these events are taking place in the state in which you intend to practice. Does your state have legislation which would change your opinion?

TASK 4:   The Federal Government has designated the lopped-ear deer as a protected species consistently for the last two decades and requires the State of Y to take necessary measures to protect the lopped-ear deer and promote its population growth. The State of Y's most recent study concluded that, in the past five years, the deer species has seen slow growth in the State of Y's southern region. The majority of lopped-ear deer reside in Beautiful State Park which borders the Double T Ranch on the park's southeastern edge. The Double T Ranch leases out large portions of the ranch to hunters during deer season. In the last two hunting seasons, State of Y game wardens have fined four hunters for shooting and killing lopped-ear deer. The Federal Government has expressed its concern that State of Y is not doing enough to protect the lopped-ear deer. Despite the game warden's threats to levy heavy fines and penalties against the Double T Ranch the next time a hunter shoots a lopped-ear deer, the ranch owners seem to show little concern for the species' welfare.

The State of Y, in conjunction with the Federal Government, would like to take possession of a section of the Double T Ranch to be included in Beautiful State Park because this area of the ranch contains a large population of lopped-ear deer. The government also wants to take a small additional "bubble" area that would allow the deer extra space to roam. Because the owners of Double T Ranch are heavy political campaign contributors, representatives of the State of Y would like this process to be as amicable as possible. However, the ranch owners are currently refusing to accept reasonable compensation to sell any part of the ranch and have indicated they would fight any attempt to take part of the ranch.

As the new attorney for the Parks and Wildlife Department, prepare a memo discussing whether the State of Y can take the property by eminent domain and how to keep a good relationship with the owners of the ranch.

APPLICABLE LAW:

§ 13.302.   Programs for the Development of Outdoor Recreation Resources

The Parks and Wildlife Department is the state agency which cooperates with the federal government in the administration of federal assistance programs for the planning, acquisition, operation, and development of the outdoor recreation resources of the state, including acquisition of land and water and interests in land and water. The department shall cooperate with the federal government in the administration of the provisions of the Land and Water Conservation Fund Act of 1965 (Public Law 88-578).

§ 21.103.   Acquiring Park Sites

(a) Except as provided in Subsection (b) of this section, the department may acquire park sites, including property already devoted to public use, by purchase, condemnation, or other manner.

(b) Except as provided in Subchapter O of Chapter 22 of this code, no real property of the state or a political subdivision of the state may be acquired without its consent.

(c) The department shall exercise the power of eminent domain in the manner prescribed by general law, including the provisions of Section 13.305 of this code.

§ 13.305.   Condemnation Proceedings

(a) The department may institute condemnation proceedings according to the laws of this state to acquire land for programs developing outdoor recreation resources under Section 13.302 of this code.

(b) Costs incurred in the exercise of eminent domain under this section for the relocation, raising, lowering, rerouting, or change in grade, or alteration in the construction of any electric transmission, telegraph, or telephone line, railroad, conduit, pole, property, facility, or pipeline are the sole expense of the department.

(c) "Sole expense" means the actual cost of the lowering, rerouting, or change in grade or alteration of construction in providing comparable replacement without enhancement of the facility, after deducting the net salvage value derived from the old facility.